NTSB/RAR-07/02
PB2007-916302
Notation 7833A
Adopted September 11, 2007

Railroad Accident Report

Derailment of Chicago Transit Authority
Train Number 220 Between Clark/Lake
and Grand/Milwaukee Stations
Chicago, Illinois
July 11, 2006

**National
Transportation
Safety Board**

490 L'Enfant Plaza, S.W.
Washington, D.C. 20594

National Transportation Safety Board. 2007. *Derailment of Chicago Transit Authority Train Number 220 Between Clark/Lake and Grand/Milwaukee Stations, Chicago, Illinois, July 11, 2006.* **Railroad Accident Report NTSB/RAR-07/02. Washington, DC.**

Abstract: On Tuesday, July 11, 2006, about 5:06 p.m., central daylight time, the last car of northbound Chicago Transit Authority Blue Line train number 220 derailed in the subway between the Clark/Lake and Grand/Milwaukee stations in downtown Chicago, Illinois. About 1,000 passengers were on board the eight-car rapid transit train. Following the derailment, the train came to a stop, and electrical arcing between the last car and the 600-volt direct current third rail generated smoke. The single operator in the lead car received a number of calls on the train intercom. The operator exited the control compartment, stepped onto the catwalk, and walked beside the train to investigate.

Electrical power was removed from the third rail and most passengers walked to an emergency exit stairway about 350 feet in front of the train that led to the street level. Some passengers had to be assisted in their evacuation by emergency responders. The Chicago Fire Department reported that 152 persons were treated and transported from the scene. There were no fatalities. Total damage exceeded $1 million.

The safety issues discussed in this report are poor track conditions, ineffective management and safety oversight, difficulty locating the train, and problems with tunnel ventilation and smoke removal.

As a result of its investigation of this accident, the National Transportation Safety Board makes recommendations to the Federal Transit Administration, the State of Illinois, the Regional Transportation Authority, the Chicago Transit Board, and the Chicago Transit Authority.

CONTENTS

ACRONYMS AND ABBREVIATIONS

AMTRAK	National Railroad Passenger Corporation
APTA	American Public Transportation Association
BART	Bay Area Rapid Transit District
CFR	*Code of Federal Regulations*
CTA	Chicago Transit Authority
CTB	Chicago Transit Board
FTA	Federal Transit Administration
LIRR	Long Island Railroad
METRA	Northeast Illinois Railroad Corporation
NYCT	New York City Transit
RTA	Regional Transportation Authority

EXECUTIVE SUMMARY

On Tuesday, July 11, 2006, about 5:06 p.m., central daylight time, the last car of northbound Chicago Transit Authority Blue Line train number 220 derailed in the subway between the Clark/Lake and Grand/Milwaukee stations in downtown Chicago, Illinois. About 1,000 passengers were on board the eight-car rapid transit train. Following the derailment, the train came to a stop, and electrical arcing between the last car and the 600-volt direct current third rail generated smoke. The single operator in the lead car received a number of calls on the train intercom. The operator exited the control compartment, stepped onto the catwalk, and walked beside the train to investigate.

Electrical power was removed from the third rail, and most passengers walked to an emergency exit stairway about 350 feet in front of the train that led to the street level. Some passengers had to be assisted in their evacuation by emergency responders. The Chicago Fire Department reported that 152 persons were treated and transported from the scene. There were no fatalities. Total damage exceeded $1 million.

The National Transportation Safety Board determines that the probable cause of the July 11, 2006, derailment of Chicago Transit Authority train number 220 in the subway in Chicago, Illinois, was the Chicago Transit Authority's ineffective management and oversight of its track inspection and maintenance program and its system safety program, which resulted in unsafe track conditions. Contributing to the accident were the Regional Transportation Authority's failure to require that action be taken by the Chicago Transit Authority to correct unsafe track conditions and the Federal Transit Administration's ineffective oversight of the Regional Transportation Authority. Contributing to the seriousness of the accident was smoke in the tunnel and the delay in removing that smoke.

As a result of its investigation of this accident, the Safety Board identified the following safety issues:

- Poor track conditions,
- Ineffective management and safety oversight,
- Difficulty locating the train, and
- Problems with tunnel ventilation and smoke removal.

As a result of its investigation of this accident, the National Transportation Safety Board makes safety recommendations to the Federal Transit Administration, the State of Illinois, the Regional Transportation Authority, the Chicago Transit Board, and the Chicago Transit Authority.

FACTUAL INFORMATION

Accident Synopsis

On Tuesday, July 11, 2006, about 5:06 p.m., central daylight time,[1] the last car of northbound[2] Chicago Transit Authority (CTA) Blue Line train number 220 derailed in the subway between the Clark/Lake and Grand/Milwaukee stations in downtown Chicago, Illinois. About 1,000 passengers were on board the eight-car rapid transit train. Following the derailment, the train came to a stop, and electrical arcing between the last car and the 600-volt direct current third rail generated smoke. The single operator in the lead car received a number of calls on the train intercom. The operator exited the control compartment, stepped onto the catwalk, and walked beside the train to investigate.

Electrical power was removed from the third rail, and most passengers walked to an emergency exit stairway about 350 feet in front of the train that led to the street level. Some passengers had to be assisted in their evacuation by emergency responders. The Chicago Fire Department reported that 152 persons were treated and transported from the scene. There were no fatalities. Total damage exceeded $1 million.

Accident Narrative

The operator of train number 220 reported for duty at the Forest Park station at 4:19 p.m., on July 11, 2006. Train number 220 consisted of eight cars. The operator's supervisor saw him before he began his work trip. The supervisor said that the operator appeared confident and prepared to operate the train. The train departed at 4:36 p.m. The operator controlled the train from the control compartment on the north end of the lead car.

The train operated normally through the Clark/Lake station. As the train left Clark/Lake and the front of it was approaching CTA station number 110+0,[3]

---

[1] Unless otherwise noted, all times in this report are central daylight time.

[2] The Blue Line track is generally aligned in a geographical north to south direction; however, the track in the area of the derailment was aligned in an east to west direction.

[3] On the CTA system, station numbers are measured in 100-foot increments. The number after the (+) mark represents distance in feet. For example, 110+56 equals 11,056 feet. The Dearborn Subway Blue Line starts at station 0+00 and extends to Station 219+00.

a warning light and audible signal in the control panel, called a blue light alarm,[4] activated, indicating a problem with one of the cars. The blue light alarm operates in conjunction with an exterior indicator light that illuminates on both sides of the problem car. The operator said that he stopped the train and attempted to determine which car was having problems by looking back through his window along the train for the exterior indicator light. He said that he was unable to see a car with the indicator light illuminated due to track curvature and limited visibility. The operator then decided that he would address the problem at the next station. As the train began to move forward, its emergency-braking mode automatically activated and brought the train to a stop.

The derailment occurred in the Dearborn Subway section of the CTA system on the northbound track between the Clark/Lake and Grand/Milwaukee stations in downtown Chicago, Illinois. Postaccident investigation revealed that only the last car of the eight-car train had derailed. The point of derailment[5] was located at station 106+53 in a slight curve[6] to the left, which was the approximate location of the rear of the train when the blue light alarm occurred. The train came to a stop in a right-hand curve about 356 feet beyond the point of derailment. (See figure 1.)

At 5:07 p.m., the operator called the CTA rail controller for the Blue Line with his portable two-way radio and informed the controller that his train had gone into emergency-braking mode. The operator began receiving calls from passengers through the railcar intercom units and exited the control compartment to investigate.

Emergency Response[7]

Postaccident testing of the first six railcars showed that the interior emergency lighting functioned normally. The last two cars could not be tested due to damage incurred in the accident.

---

[4] A *blue light alarm* indicates that one of the cars in the train has a propulsion or auxiliary power problem. In the event of a blue light alarm, a trouble light illuminates on the operator's console, and an alarm bell sounds in the cab. The normal procedure is to reset the alarm. If the alarm does not reset, the operator stops the train at the next platform to inspect the car.

[5] The point of derailment was determined by examining the derailment footprint, including marks on the ties, the track components, and the rail; car and truck component positions; and broken track components.

[6] The curvature was a 2° left-hand curve. The CTA designates this curve as curve No. 104-C. It has a length of 366.88 feet and a radius of 2864.84 feet.

[7] The following sequence of emergency response events was developed from interviews and various Chicago Police Department, Chicago Fire Department, and CTA records.

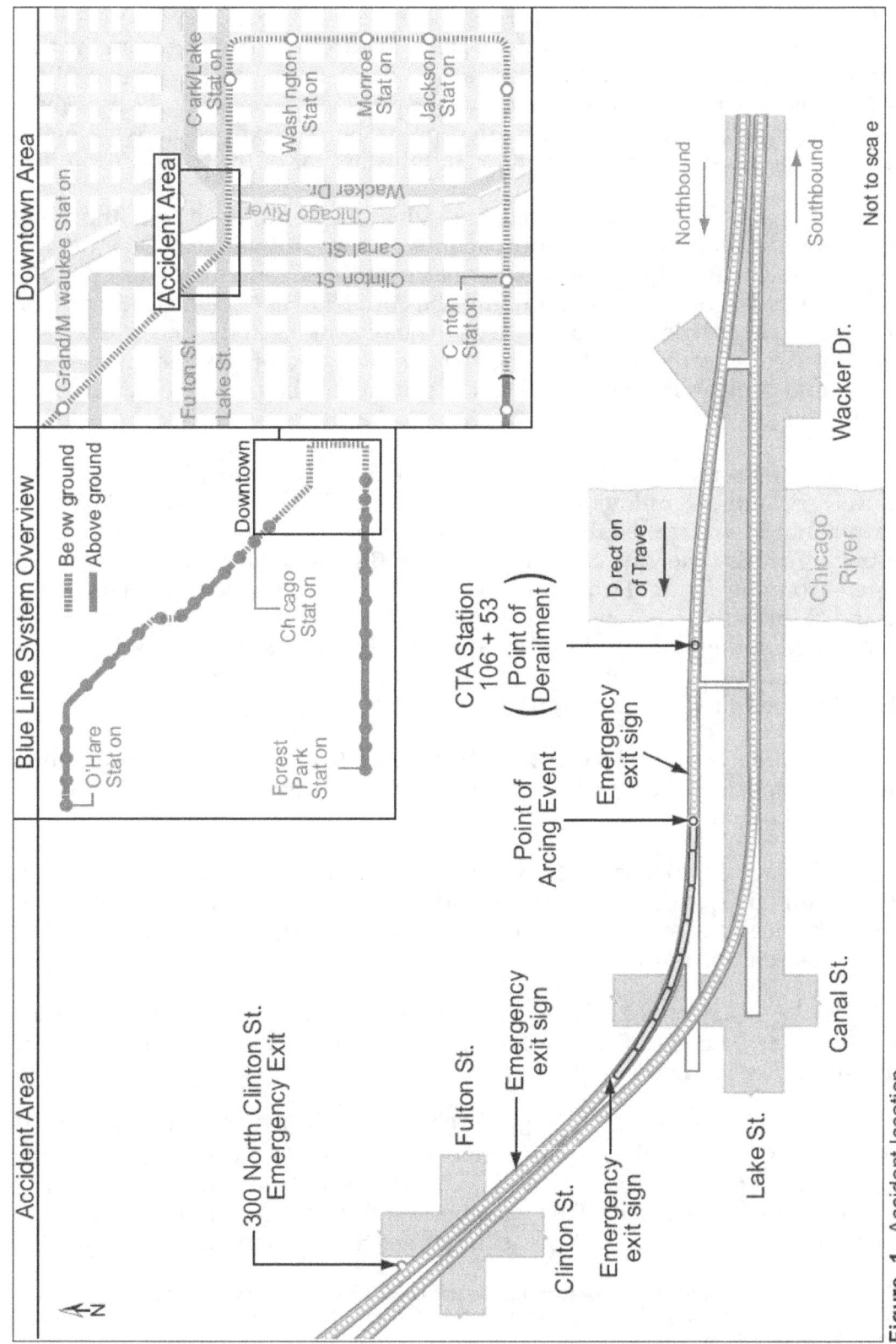

Figure 1. Accident location.

The operator exited the control compartment, stepped onto the catwalk, and walked beside the train to investigate. He noticed smoke coming from the rear of the train and moving toward the lead car. As he walked toward the rear of the train, the smoke got thicker. He saw emergency door lights on several cars, which indicated that the doors were open. At that point, he noticed people walking on the catwalk. One person told the operator that the last car of the train was on fire.

At 5:07 p.m., the operator called the rail controller and said his train had stopped while it was northbound approaching Grand/Milwaukee. The operator then went to each car with closed doors, instructed someone inside to open the doors, and helped people get out and onto the catwalk. He told those already on the catwalk to wait for him to lead, but, due to heavy smoke at the end of the train, many kept walking north away from the last car in an attempt to find an exit. The operator found himself in the middle of the group and began verbally directing them along the catwalk.

About 5:09 p.m., the CTA power controller noted anomalies on the Blue Line in the area of the derailment and manually shut down power to that section. This power shutdown affected the operation of several other trains, stopping them on the track. At this time, one caller informed a 911 dispatcher that he and other passengers from the accident train were on the Blue Line between the Clark/Lake and Grand/Milwaukee stations, and that the train was on fire and there was a lot of smoke. Another caller told a 911 dispatcher that the train's location was between Washington and Grand underground. Fire department companies were dispatched to the Clark/Lake station for a train fire.

At 5:10 p.m., a police officer was dispatched to the Clark/Lake station in response to a reported train crash. The CTA power controller notified its units of a problem on the Blue Line.

The Chicago Fire Department initially dispatched four engine companies, four truck companies, one heavy rescue squad, one command and communications unit, five advanced life support ambulances, and one mobile ventilation unit[8] to the Clark/Lake station entrance.

At 5:12 p.m., a police officer informed his dispatcher that there was no smoke at the Clark/Lake station and that he had been told the accident was at the Grand/Milwaukee station.

At 5:13 p.m., according to the CTA's Supervisory Control and Data Acquisition logs, a door alarm was activated at the 300 North Clinton Street emergency exit. At 5:14 p.m., a passenger called 911 and said that she just came out of an exit at Clinton Street. This was the first 911 call from a passenger at an emergency exit on street level. Also at this time, the power controller activated

---

[8] The Chicago Fire Department deployed its mobile ventilation unit to nearby ventilation shafts identified by its *Subway Response Manual*. The mobile ventilation unit is capable of exhausting smoke out of large structures, including the subway tunnels.

the emergency lights and announcements system at two emergency exits near the Grand/Milwaukee station.

At 5:15 p.m., a passenger still in the subway used emergency call box 52379 to call for help. The caller spoke with the CTA power controller who tried to determine where the caller was located. The caller provided the call box identification number, but the power controller said that the number did not give him the caller's location. The power controller told the caller that he had activated the emergency lights and announcements system at the exits.[9] Shortly thereafter, the caller told the power controller that he and the other passengers with him had found an exit (at 300 North Clinton Street).

At 5:16 p.m., a police officer told his dispatcher that he was at the Grand/ Milwaukee station and that there was no train or smoke at that location. The police dispatcher then told the officer that according to the CTA there was no train crash, but there was smoke in the tunnel. At this point, several Chicago Fire Department units had been directed to the Grand/Milwaukee station. Also at this time, an ambulance was directed to 300 North Clinton Street in response to reports of people coming out of the emergency exit. Several other Chicago Fire Department units that initially responded to the Clark/Lake and Grand/Milwaukee stations were also redirected to the emergency exit at 300 North Clinton Street.

At 5:18 p.m., while these initial response efforts were being orchestrated above ground, the operator was walking in the tunnel with the passengers that had evacuated the train when he saw a sign indicating there was an exit 200 feet north of them. (This was the CTA's 300 North Clinton Street emergency exit.) The operator informed the group of the direction and distance to the exit, and they moved toward it.

At this point, several other rush hour trains were stalled on the Blue Line tracks, and passengers were evacuating from each of the trains. At 5:19 p.m., the rail controller called 911 and asked for assistance evacuating people at the Grand/ Milwaukee station. The controller also indicated that there was a train emitting smoke and that there were a lot of people coming out of the Grand/Milwaukee and Chicago stations.

About 5:20 p.m., the surveillance video pointing into the northbound tunnel at the Lake/Wells entrance to the Clark/Lake station recorded smoke at the bend in the tunnel. At 5:22 p.m., the CTA began evacuating the passengers from other trains onto the platform and up the Clark/Lake station stairs. Also, a caller on the phone with a 911 dispatcher reported a fire on the CTA system. He said that he was at Fulton and Clinton (the 300 North Clinton Street emergency exit) and that an ambulance had just arrived.

---

[9] These were the 655 and 881 North Milwaukee Avenue exits, located north of the 300 North Clinton Street exit.

At 5:24 p.m., smoke entered the Clark/Lake station platform area. Also, the power controller activated the emergency lights and announcements system at the 300 North Clinton Street emergency exit.

At 5:25 p.m., a caller told a 911 dispatcher that she was stuck at the bottom of the "L," that there was a really big fire, and that she had not seen the fire department. At 5:33 p.m., a caller on the phone with a 911 dispatcher said that firefighters were on the scene and in the tunnel.

At 5:43 p.m., the Chicago Fire Department directed additional resources to the 300 North Clinton Street emergency exit. All passengers from the accident train exited the tunnel at this location. In spite of the buildup of heavy smoke at the emergency exit, the operator remained in the tunnel and directed the rest of the passengers out.

At 5:49 p.m., firefighters reported that they had located the fire and were conducting a second search of the train. They requested portable extinguishers from fire personnel outside. By this time, all the passengers and the operator had exited the tunnel.

The Chicago Fire Department forward commander supervised the operations in the tunnel for passenger evacuation, search and rescue, and fire suppression. He and additional firefighters entered the tunnel through the emergency exit as passengers exited. They encountered smoke as soon as they entered the tunnel. According to the forward commander, the evacuation seemed orderly and without panic. He reported that two passengers fell from the catwalk and needed assistance to exit the tunnel. Firefighters assisted one other passenger from the tunnel.

Firefighters used a pressurized water extinguisher and a dry chemical extinguisher to put out a smoldering fire on the underside of the train. By 6:00 p.m., the Clark/Lake platform was clear of smoke. Firefighters conducted numerous searches of the tunnel to confirm that all passengers had exited. At 6:21 p.m., an additional heavy rescue squad was dispatched to assist with the searches in the tunnel. At 9:41 p.m., the Chicago Fire Department returned control of the subway to the CTA.

In total, the Chicago Fire Department on-scene resources included 28 ambulances, 15 engine companies, 9 truck companies, 3 mass casualty units, 1 hazardous material unit, 2 specialized rescue squads, 1 advanced life support bicycle team, 1 mobile ventilation unit, 1 air mask unit, a helicopter, 2 mobile command posts, and additional command staff.

Injuries

The Chicago Fire Department reported that 152 persons were treated and transported from the scene, including 3 injured firefighters and 1 injured CTA supervisor. There were no fatalities. Hospital records indicate that 6 passengers suffered serious injuries[10] and 21 passengers sustained minor injuries as a result of the post-derailment smoke and evacuation. The majority of injuries were due to smoke inhalation.

Damage

Equipment

Postaccident examination revealed that except for the car that derailed, all of the other cars in the accident train were in excellent condition. The last car of the eight-car train had extensive damage to the current collector assembly[11] on its left side. The forward portion of the pickup shoe and its supporting structure were missing. The remaining section was heavily melted. The insulator material for the current collector assembly showed heavy thermal damage and large areas of missing material. The insulating support beam for the assembly was broken with missing material that appeared to have been consumed by electrical arcing. The fiberglass flash shield for the assembly also had been consumed. The electrical cabling to the assembly had its insulation burned away and the cable was brittle. The stainless steel sidewall of the car located directly above the current collector assembly was white, chalky, and buckled by heat. Electrical arcing also caused other areas of minor damage on equipment under the car. The CTA estimated that the cost of the damaged railroad equipment exceeded $970,000.

Track and Structures

Postaccident examination revealed that multiple rail fastener devices (lag screws, rail clip assemblies, and tie plates) for the outer rail in the curve at CTA station 106+53 had been corroded, worn, bent, broken, and/or displaced from their associated half-ties,[12] and the rail had moved laterally outward under load. (See figure 2.)

---

[10] Title 49 *Code of Federal Regulations* 830.2 defines fatal injury as "any injury which results in death within 30 days of the accident" and *serious injury* as "an injury which: (1) requires hospitalization for more than 48 hours, commencing within 7 days from the date the injury was received; (2) results in a fracture of any bone (except simple fractures of fingers, toes, or nose); (3) causes severe hemorrhages, nerve, or tendon damage; (4) involves any internal organ; or (5) involves second or third-degree burns, or any burn affecting more than 5 percent of the body surface."

[11] The *current collector assembly* is a combination mechanical and electrical device that transfers electricity from the third rail through the pickup shoe to the train cars to power the electrical motors.

[12] A *half-tie* measures 30 inches long by 8 1/2 inches wide by 7 inches deep. A full tie typically measures 8 1/2 feet long. The smaller size of the half-tie is meant to facilitate water drainage on the tunnel floor.

Figure 2. Outside rail of curve near point of derailment.

In the area of the derailment, a 9-inch-long by 3-inch-deep section of the steel electrified third rail[13] was consumed by arcing. The aluminum strip usually attached to the rail was also consumed. The material surrounding the missing section of the electrified third rail was heavily melted and pitted.

The concrete wall by the gap in the electrified third rail exhibited clean burn[14] in a circular area, several feet in diameter, at ground level. The concrete pad underneath the rail was spalled[15] in the heat-affected area.

Parts of the adjacent signal system were destroyed by the wheels of the derailed car. In addition, the signal cable conduit that ran under the track and up the wall of the tunnel catwalk had been torn loose and the cable had been severed.

The CTA reported that track and signal damage in the area of the derailment was about $34,900.

---

[13] The *third rail* is 74-pounds-per-yard aluminum clad contact rail. It is made of steel with an aluminum strip attached to each side of the rail to improve conduction. The rail is 5 3/16 inches in height and the widest part of the railhead is 2 9/16 inches. The base of the rail is 4 inches wide.

[14] *Clean burn* is a fire pattern on a surface where the soot has been burned away.

[15] *Spalling* is the chipping or pitting of concrete or masonry surfaces. It can be caused by exposure to high temperatures.

Train and Operations Information

The CTA is the second largest public transit system in the United States. Its rail system has 224 miles of track and 144 stations used for passenger service. In 2006, on a daily basis during the workweek about 500,000 riders were transported on the system.

The Chicago Transit Board (CTB) governs and administers the CTA. The CTB consists of members appointed by the Governor of Illinois and the Mayor of Chicago, subject to various approvals. The CTB is responsible for overseeing transit facility operations.

CTA trains operate 7 days a week, 24 hours a day. Rush hours are from 6:00 a.m. to 9:00 a.m. and from 3:00 p.m. to 7:00 p.m. During these hours, trains run about 4 minutes apart. From 9:00 a.m. to 3:00 p.m. and from 7:00 p.m. to midnight, trains run about 7 minutes apart. For two short periods just after midnight and just before 6:00 a.m. trains run about 15 minutes apart. During the rest of the early morning hours, the trains run about every 30 minutes.[16]

The derailment occurred on the CTA's Blue Line. The Blue Line is controlled by automatic block signals and time controlled signals, and it has 33 stops, including the first at the Forest Park station and the last at the O'Hare station. A single operator controls each train. The maximum authorized speed through the area of the derailment was 25 mph; no slow zones were posted.

The CTA provided train derailment analysis documentation from 2001 through 2006. There had been seven derailments attributed to track conditions during this period, not including this derailment. None of the seven accidents involved track conditions similar to that involved in this accident. Two of the seven accidents involved revenue passenger trains on the mainline track; the others involved trains on yard tracks.

The train involved in the derailment consisted of eight cars. The cars were designed to run in four semi-permanently coupled, or "married," pairs. There was a control stand at either end of each pair. The outside ends of each married pair were identified as the #1 ends and the coupled ends of each pair were identified as the #2 ends. Individual cars were 48 feet long and 9 feet 4 inches wide, and each

---

[16] The CTA reported the following daily average train frequencies over the derailment area: 52 4-car trains and 143 8-car trains on weekdays, 157 4-car trains on Saturdays, and 128 4-car trains on Sundays. Using these frequencies, the annual train traffic over this area equals 16.4 million gross tons.

had two two-axle trucks with traction motor powered axles. The cars involved in the derailment were not equipped with event recorders.[17, 18]

The railcars were designed to run using a 600-volt direct current provided by an electrically energized third rail located just outside and parallel to the running rails. Within the tunnels, the interior configuration and safety considerations dictated the placement of the third rail, and it was installed on either the right or left side of the track. Each car had a low voltage (36-volt direct current) system used to control functions within the car, such as lighting, the intercom, and door movement. A battery bank underneath each car provided electricity to the low voltage system during power interruptions.

On the exterior sides of each car is a vertical row of four indicator lights. The top light shows red when the doors are open. The next lower light shows yellow when the friction brakes are applied. The next lower light shows blue whenever any one of 31 malfunction events occur in the electrical motor or control system. The bottom light shows green when the doors close properly.

Personnel Information

Operator

Train 220 was controlled by a single operator. The operator was hired by the CTA on March 7, 2005. He qualified on the Green Line on May 27, 2005, and on the Blue Line on July 8, 2006. He was trained in accordance with CTA standards.

The operator told investigators that he was not taking any prescription or non-prescription medications. Breath and urine specimens were collected from the operator in accordance with Federal postaccident toxicological testing regulations. The specimens were collected on July 11, 2006, at 9:01 p.m. All specimens tested negative for the presence of drugs and alcohol. Company records and interviews did not indicate any medical problems that would affect normal operations or duties.

---

[17] According to the CTA, none of the railcars in its present fleet are equipped with event recorders. New cars scheduled for delivery in 2009 will be equipped with event recorders.

[18] As a result of two similar rear-end train collisions that occurred within a 2-month period on the CTA system in 2001, the Safety Board issued Safety Recommendation R-02-19 to the Federal Transit Administration (FTA): "Require that new or rehabilitated vehicles funded by Federal Transit Administration grants be equipped with event recorders meeting Institute of Electrical and Electronics Engineers Standard 1482.1 for rail transit vehicle event recorders." The Board has asked that the FTA reconsider its position of providing information and guidance and instead take measures to require that new or rehabilitated vehicles funded by FTA grants be equipped with event recorders. Safety Recommendation R-02-19 is classified "Open—Unacceptable Response" pending FTA action on this issue.

Track Inspectors

The CTA track inspection team for the portion of the Blue Line in the Dearborn Subway section that included the point of derailment consisted of two inspectors. One track inspector, Inspector A, was hired by the CTA on October 9, 2000. He had spent   3 months working in a construction crew, and he had worked as a track inspector for more than 5 years. He had been responsible for inspecting track in the Dearborn Subway tunnel for the 3 years prior to the accident.

The other track inspector, Inspector B, was hired by the CTA on April 28, 1998. He had worked in various construction crews cleaning track for 1 1/2 years and delivering and picking up track material for another 5 years before becoming a track inspector in August 2004. His initial track inspector job involved inspecting ballasted track structure in daylight conditions until May 2005 when he was injured. He returned to track inspection in December 2005 and was assigned to inspect track in the tunnels. About 4 months before the derailment, he began inspecting tracks in the Dearborn Subway tunnel.

Section Roadmaster

The section roadmaster was hired by the CTA on June 9, 1975. He worked on a track gang installing and maintaining track for 10 years, as a track inspector for 10 years, and as a section roadmaster for 11 years. He was temporarily assigned the territory that included the Dearborn Subway tunnel on January 27, 2006, about 5 months before the accident. He supervised about 16 track inspectors, including those responsible for the section of the Blue Line where the derailment occurred. He was filling in for the regular roadmaster that had been temporarily assigned to work with construction crews.

Track Information

Structure

Investigators examined the accident site and found that a major portion of the track structure was directly fixed to the wood half-ties, which were embedded in the concrete subway floor. (See figure 3.) The half-ties' centerlines were spaced 2 feet apart. Placed on top of the half-ties were 7 3/4-inch by 12-inch tie plates. These tie plates were primarily fastened to the half-ties with lag screws.[19] The rail was fastened to the tie plates with spring clips. The rail was 100 pound[20] jointed rail manufactured in Illinois in 1948. Most track components were original equipment and had been in place since the track was constructed in 1951.

---

[19]   There were some locations where track maintenance employees added 6-inch "cut" track spikes.

[20]   A rail section weighing 100.25 pounds per yard of rail.

Figure 3. Chicago Transit Authority subway tunnel in derailment area, showing mud and water conditions.

Track Inspection

The CTA performed visual track inspections twice a week to determine if the track conditions were safe for the posted speed. The inspections consisted of observing track defects and comparing them with the rating categories established in CTA's *Track Maintenance Standards Manual* for the various posted speeds. Prior to the derailment, the Track Department did not utilize a track geometry vehicle[21] or internal rail defect detector equipment[22] to complement the track inspectors' visual inspections.[23]

The CTA Track Department consists of section crews and construction crews. The section crews perform inspections and repairs. The construction crews perform the heavy maintenance and construction work, which includes changing ties and rail and installing new track. The CTA required teams of two inspectors to visually inspect the track by walking within the confines of the track. Each track inspector had a flashlight. In addition, the inspectors used a tapeline ruler to

---

[21] A track geometry vehicle is capable of a continuous loaded measurement of gage, track cross level, track alignment, track warp, and ride quality.

[22] Rail defect detector equipment is capable of scanning the rail for internal defect growth. The General Manager of Power and Way Engineering stated that the track department performs a "Soni Rail" joint inspection annually, in which the rail in the joint area is inspected for bolthole cracks.

[23] A survey of several other transit agencies and passenger railroads revealed that they all utilized track geometry vehicles and rail defect detection equipment to supplement the visual track inspections. (See "Industry Track Inspector Qualifications and Training" in this report.)

measure potential track deficiencies and a note pad, pen, and chalk to identify the location and type of those deficiencies.

There were 69 track inspectors systemwide. The CTA required[24] that all mainline tracks be inspected twice a week with at least 2 calendar days between inspections. In general, the track inspectors inspected the track on Mondays and Thursdays. On Tuesdays and Fridays, they made minor repairs on the track defects that they had found on the previous inspection day. On Wednesdays, all the track inspectors of a given territory worked together on maintenance projects and larger defective track conditions that were found within their territory.

All CTA track inspectors typically worked from 7:00 a.m. to 3:30 p.m. Because of rush hour train traffic in the morning and in the afternoon, track inspectors could not start their inspections until 9:00 a.m. and had to be off the track by 3:00 p.m. In this accident, the two inspectors responsible for the track inspections between the Chicago and Clinton stations, which included the area of the derailment, reported for work about 7:00 a.m.

Track Conditions

Both track inspectors said that they had observed tie plate and fastener corrosion and water damaged half-ties in the area where the derailment occurred. However, they had not detected rail movement or gage problems. Inspector A stated that he did report the tie condition to his section roadmaster,[25] but there was no tie replacement work conducted in the area of the derailment. Gage rods[26] had been installed at locations 45 and 75 feet north and 120 and 135 feet south of the derailment area.

The section roadmaster said that in the 5 months he had been responsible for the territory where the derailment had occurred, he had inspected the tunnel area with his immediate supervisor, the Track Engineer IV Maintenance,[27] and the Manager of Track. He noted that they all agreed that "the area was bad," but that the staff was not available to make the permanent repairs. The Track Engineer IV Maintenance and the Manager of Track did not recall this inspection or the discussion. The Manager of Track said he was aware that many of the half-ties and tie plates in the tunnel needed replacement.

---

[24] *Track Maintenance Standard Manual*, Requirement 102, "Track Inspection Requirements."

[25] The track inspector could not recall the date when he reported the tie condition to the section roadmaster on his inspection sheet. He said that it had been more than a year prior to the accident.

[26] A *gage rod* is a temporary repair device used to maintain the track gage. It consists of a 1 1/4-inch-diameter threaded rod with a forged jaw on one end and a malleable jaw on the other end. The length is adjusted with a locknut.

[27] *Track Engineer IV Maintenance* is an official title. This position reports to the Manager of Track. It is generally, but unofficially, referred to by other employees as a general foreman or a general roadmaster.

The Manager of Track observed the track conditions immediately after the derailment. He stated that he noticed a lot of water and mud around the base of the rail and the tie plates. He also saw corroded tie plates, screw spikes, and track spikes. He believed that an electrolysis process had corroded the metal away from the tie plates, and as the train moved through the curve, the rail on the high side of the curve shifted outward.

In a 2005 budget presentation, the General Manager for Power and Way Maintenance proposed that the priorities for track maintenance in the Dearborn Subway were to replace wood half-ties with concrete slabs and replace the rail. As part of the presentation, an example of a tie plate that had corroded after only 1 year in service was shown. In 2005, construction crews had begun replacing defective wood half-ties on the northbound track in the Dearborn Subway. In the 2 years before the derailment, about 400 to 500 of the defective wood half-ties were replaced with concrete slabs with permanently affixed tie plates. The tie replacement area was approximately 1 mile north of the derailment site.

Postaccident Walking Inspections

After the accident, a walking track inspection was conducted in the immediate area of the derailment. The inspection found that some areas of the tunnel floor were wet and there were areas of standing water. In addition, there were wet and rotten half-ties, and mud and debris covered some drainage areas. Water had seeped onto the track structure from the tunnel wall seams.

The inspection found that the base of the rail and the rail fastener system (the tie plates, the lag screws, and the spring clips) had corrosion damage. In some areas, track spikes had been added in conjunction with lag screws, and where spring clips or lag screws were missing, track spikes had been used instead.[28] There was also evidence of both rail and tie plate movement on the half-ties. (See figure 4.)

Postaccident track geometry measurements included gage and cross level measurements. The outside rail in the curve was the reference rail for cross level measurements. The CTA's optimum gage measurement is 56 1/2 inches.

At the point of derailment, the rails appeared to be spread from the dynamics of the derailment, and the gage equaled 60 1/4 inches. Measurements were taken north and south of the point of derailment on track where the rail fastener system appeared to be intact, indicating that the rail in these areas had not been affected by the derailment. The gage 15 1/2 feet south of the point of derailment equaled 58 1/8 inches, and the gage 15 1/2 feet north of the point of derailment equaled 58 inches.

---

[28] *Track spikes* compromise the electrical isolation of the rail.

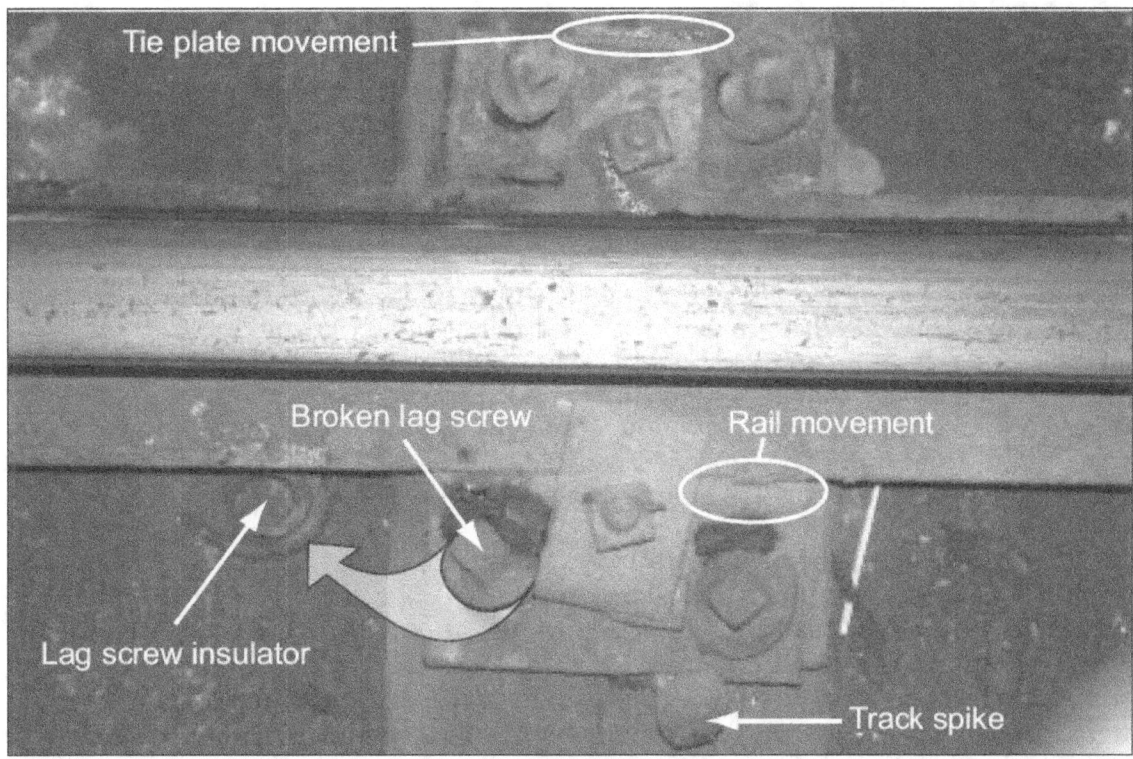

Figure 4. Tie plate and rail movement of outside rail near point of derailment. Large white arrow shows displacement of insulator from broken lag screw.

The CTA *Track Maintenance Standards Manual* Requirement 301, "Track Gage," establishes track gage requirements. Requirement 105, "Track Rating Criteria for Establishing Allowable Speeds," specifies that a maximum allowable speed of 6 mph be placed on a track gage equal to 58 inches, and that track gages above 58 inches be placed out of service.

Investigators found dark streaks[29] on the inner rail (low rail) *of the curve.* CTA Requirement 302, "Gage Problems," establishes some possible indications that a track gage problem exists. These include dark streaks on the low rail of a curve, lateral movement of tie plate on the tie or rail on the tie plate, missing spikes, and poor tie conditions.

A second postaccident walking inspection was conducted between 9:00 a.m. and 3:00 p.m. to examine the amount of time available to complete an inspection of the territory and the working conditions encountered during a routine track inspection.[30]

---

[29] *Dark streaks* indicate an absence of wheel to rail contact. According to the CTA *Track Maintenance Standards Manual*, such dark areas are a leading indicator of wide gage track conditions.

[30] This inspection team included a Safety Board investigator and one of the CTA track inspectors responsible for this territory.

Factors such as the length of track to be inspected in the 6.22-mile territory[31] and the train density were considered. The walking inspection tried to mirror a routine track inspection. The inspection found that the tunnel lighting was not sufficient to light the track structure, so a flashlight was used to simultaneously observe walking conditions and look for track deficiencies. Once a train was heard and/or sighted, the inspectors had to clear the track. To do this required carefully stepping over the exposed 600-volt third rail and standing against the tunnel wall. Once against the wall, the inspectors signaled the oncoming train operator by flashlight to slow the train down to about 6 mph. Once the train passed, the third rail had to be traversed again, and the track inspection continued.

When a track deficiency was noted during the inspection, measurements or observations were recorded on a note card for later transcription to an inspection report, and the tunnel wall and rail were marked with chalk to help identify the exact location of the track deficiency.

Around noon, the inspectors ascended the passenger platform of the nearest station and took a train to the downtown State of Illinois Building for lunch. The round trip ride and meal took about an hour, after which the inspection of the track resumed. As the time neared 2:45 p.m., the track inspection stopped, and the inspectors got off at the nearest passenger platform and caught a train back to the CTA Tower. This routine was consistent with a normal inspection day. There was not enough time to inspect the entire territory; the inspectors were unable to inspect about 1.5 miles of the 6.22-mile distance.

After this postaccident walking inspection, the CTA track inspector stated that they typically did not finish inspecting their entire territory in a single day. He said that the inspection reports were completed showing the entire length of the territory even though only part of the territory may have been inspected.

Track Inspection Records

The initial review of track inspection records for the Blue Line territory that included the derailment area revealed that more than 80 percent of the records for the time between May 1 and July 11, 2006, were missing. These deficiencies prompted a more detailed examination of the CTA track inspection records for all territories for the 12-month period prior to the accident. This examination revealed the following:

- Hundreds of inspection records were not available.

- No track inspection territory had records that documented every inspection required by the CTA. (The CTA required two inspections a week for the 12-month period.)

---

[31] The inspection territory was about 3.11 miles one way. A routine inspection required independently examining both the northbound and southbound tracks.

- Eight inspection territories had large time periods, a month or more, with no records. Five of these eight inspection territories had 3- to 4-month periods with no records.

- Many of the records that were provided were not filled out correctly. Examples of irregularities included not identifying the track inspected and not signing or dating the record.

- Many records identified defects, but there were no parallel records that demonstrated that repairs were made to correct the defects.

- Although inspection reports indicated that the full length of territory had been inspected, multiple track defects were concentrated in certain areas while no defects were noted in the remainder of the territory.

Oversight of Track Inspections

First level supervision is provided by section roadmasters. A section roadmaster is responsible for a given territory and several track inspection teams. A section roadmaster communicates with track inspectors in person or by telephone each morning and issues work assignments. Throughout the day, a section roadmaster communicates with track inspectors via portable radio. A section roadmaster is responsible for the quality and completeness of the track inspectors' work. In addition, CTA Requirement 102 states that a section roadmaster must make a general inspection of all assigned territory once a month; no written records are required.

The section roadmaster supervising the inspectors in the area of the derailment stated that he had just enough track inspectors to cover each particular inspection territory. However, in the event that an inspector was absent from work, the inspection would not take place. In addition, if an important maintenance situation occurred, he would halt the inspections and utilize the inspectors to make the necessary repairs. He said that his track inspectors did not work overtime to finish the required weekly inspections. The section roadmaster stated that he did not always conduct a monthly inspection of his territory. In fact, he had only inspected the tracks in his territory once in the 5 months before the derailment. However, the track inspectors for the area of the derailment said that the section roadmaster would show up and help determine what remedial action was necessary when they requested help.

Oversight of the section roadmasters was the responsibility of the Track Engineer IV Maintenance. However, he said that he spent most of his time ordering track materials for all of his section roadmasters. The Track Engineer IV Maintenance for the area of the derailment managed five section roadmasters. He said that he did not review the track inspectors' inspection reports because that was the responsibility of his roadmasters. The Track Engineer IV Maintenance reports to the Manager of Track.

The Manager of Track stated that the number of maintenance personnel in his department had declined due to budgetary constraints since January 2001, when he began working in his present position. He noted that this had not affected the number of track inspectors because they are required to have two inspectors for each inspection area. He also said that the roadmasters were still responsible for the quality and completeness of the track inspections. He further noted that he expected the tracks to be completely inspected twice per week as required, even if that entailed the inspectors working overtime and on Saturdays.

System Safety Oversight

The CTA utilized a System Safety Program Plan approach to monitor and inspect the varying functions of its responsible departments. The System Safety Program Plan delineated the responsibilities for the department managers that were monitored by System Safety personnel. For example, one of the responsibilities of the Vice President, Engineering was the following:

> Ensures appropriate preventative maintenance, repair and renewal to secure the integrity of structure, track, signal and traction power conversion and distribution systems. Maintains equipment and infrastructure within all applicable government standards, equipment specifications and in accordance with the Facilities Maintenance Plan.

The System Safety personnel were not required to monitor the track structure, and they did not have technical track expertise. They also did not review track inspection records. The System Safety personnel stated that they primarily concentrated on the walkway areas in the tunnels and emergency exits, and left the oversight of track inspection to the track department. They further added that they conducted their inspections from the walkways and on the station platforms.[32]

CTA Track Inspector Qualifications and Training

CTA Requirement 103, "Qualifications of Track Inspectors," states:

> All track inspectors shall have a minimum of one-year experience in track and must have passed the applicable maintenance standards class. All inspectors must have and maintain the department criteria for advancements. All inspectors must also be approved to inspect track by the section Roadmaster for the assigned territory.

---

[32] The annual Subway Safety Audit for the Dearborn Subway conducted on November 15, 2005, reflected items that needed to be addressed, such as inspecting and/or replacing fire extinguishers; disposing of burnt out light bulbs; and repairing broken door locks, an inoperable emergency phone, and a clogged drain between the running rails.

The General Manager of Power and Way Maintenance stated that track inspector training is a two-part process. The first part was a 1-day course in a classroom setting, where both the *Track Maintenance Standards Manual* and on-track safety were taught to a new track employee. The class instructors discussed the written material relevant for conducting thorough track inspections and procedures for coding track defects. This material included the *Roadmaster's Training Program, Track Maintenance Inspection, and the Track Maintenance Standards Manual*. The *Track Maintenance Standards Manual* listed 16 possible indications of a gage problem, including dark streaks on the inside rail of a curve, lateral movement of tie plate on the tie or rail on the tie plate, missing spikes, and poor tie conditions. The classroom training did not cover procedures for inspections conducted in a tunnel or on an elevated structure, nor did it address problems associated with electrolysis and corrosion.

In the second part of the track inspector training, the trainee was placed in a construction crew for about 1 year. This was intended to familiarize the trainee with track tools and track maintenance procedures. The construction crews usually conducted larger maintenance projects, including cross-tie replacement, rail replacement, cleaning, delivering materials, and switch replacement. The trainee may then be sent to a section to become a track inspector and to work with an experienced track inspector to gain on-the-job training.

Both track inspectors responsible for the area of the derailment had successfully completed CTA's track inspection and safety training.[33] Inspector B said that he felt the 1-day class covered too much material in a short period of time for him to feel confident performing inspections. He said that he gained most of his knowledge about track inspections through on-the-job training with his track inspection partner, Inspector A.

Inspector B told investigators that he understood the written material describing gage problems. He also said that he had the knowledge and ability to successfully detect and repair wide gage. In fact, the two track inspectors had previously detected wide gage problems and corroded track structures during their regular track inspections. They reported these incidents of wide gage or corrosion and repaired them when they could. They had not documented the location of the derailment as a problem area.

Inspector B did say that detecting gage problems is more difficult inside a tunnel because it is darker, and an inspector cannot see as far down the tracks to observe varying rail gage alignments. He also said that corrosion is more common inside a tunnel than outside. Moreover, portions of track inside a tunnel may be covered in water or mud, making it more difficult to assess the gage and to detect corrosion.

---

[33] Inspector A had prior railroad experience and only worked in a construction crew for 3 months. Inspector B worked in a construction crew for 6 1/2 years before becoming a track inspector.

Industry Track Inspector Qualifications and Training

CTA procedures were compared to those of two other transit agencies, the Bay Area Rapid Transit District (BART) and New York City Transit (NYCT), and three passenger railroads regulated by the Federal Railroad Administration, the Long Island Railroad (LIRR), the National Railroad Passenger Corporation (AMTRAK), and the Northeast Illinois Railroad Corporation (METRA). The investigation attempted to determine how track inspectors are selected, how they maintain their proficiency, and how they demonstrate that they are retaining their knowledge in the other systems.

The comparison indicated that track inspector positions at the other transit agencies and railroads required more experience and training in the track discipline than the positions at the CTA. Applicants apply for a track inspection position, which is granted based on seniority and qualifications. For example, at the NYCT, before a track worker can apply for a track inspector's assignment, the track worker must pass the required training and work as a track inspector on a trial basis for at least 1 year. During that year, the track worker serves as the track inspector whenever the regular track inspector is absent and does maintenance activities as needed. At BART, an applicant must have a minimum of 3 years of experience within the track department to be considered for a track inspector's position. At AMTRAK, LIRR, and METRA, track inspectors must have experience as a track foreman.

Training programs are more extensive at the other transit agencies and railroads examined for this investigation. At the NYCT, a track inspector's training is initially 4 weeks long, and within 6 months the inspector returns for 1 additional week of training. At BART, initial classroom training is typically 40 hours and track inspectors return for the training annually. At AMTRAK, a track inspector initially receives 176 hours of classroom training. At LIRR, a track inspector initially receives 160 hours of classroom training. At METRA, the initial training is only about 48 hours, but the worker will take training several times before becoming a track inspector. All of these transit agencies and railroads have yearly recurrent training scheduled on specific subject matter, such as continuous welded rail requirements, and every 2 to 3 years thereafter on all subject matter covered during initial training. AMTRAK, LIRR, and METRA also require proficiency in their own track standards in addition to the requirements in "Designation of Qualified Persons to Supervise Certain Renewals and Inspect Track" in 49 *Code of Federal Regulations* (CFR) 213.7.

Materials Laboratory Examination

The lag screws, spring clips, tie plates, insulators, and wood tie core samples from the area of the derailment were examined at the Safety Board's Materials Laboratory. All metal components were covered with orange and black oxides. Ten of the 12 lag screws examined had fractured. Each of the 10 lag screws had significant metal loss due to corrosion and/or wear that caused a reduction in their diameter. Nine of the lag screws fractured in the corroded areas corresponding to the lag screws' upper threads. The fracture on the 10th lag screw occurred in an area of reduced diameter that corresponded to wear from contact with the associated tie plate. Eight of the 12 lag screws had similar reductions in diameter that corresponded to wear from contact with a tie plate. (See figure 5.) Insulators were installed between the lag screws and the tie plates and should have prevented contact between the two.

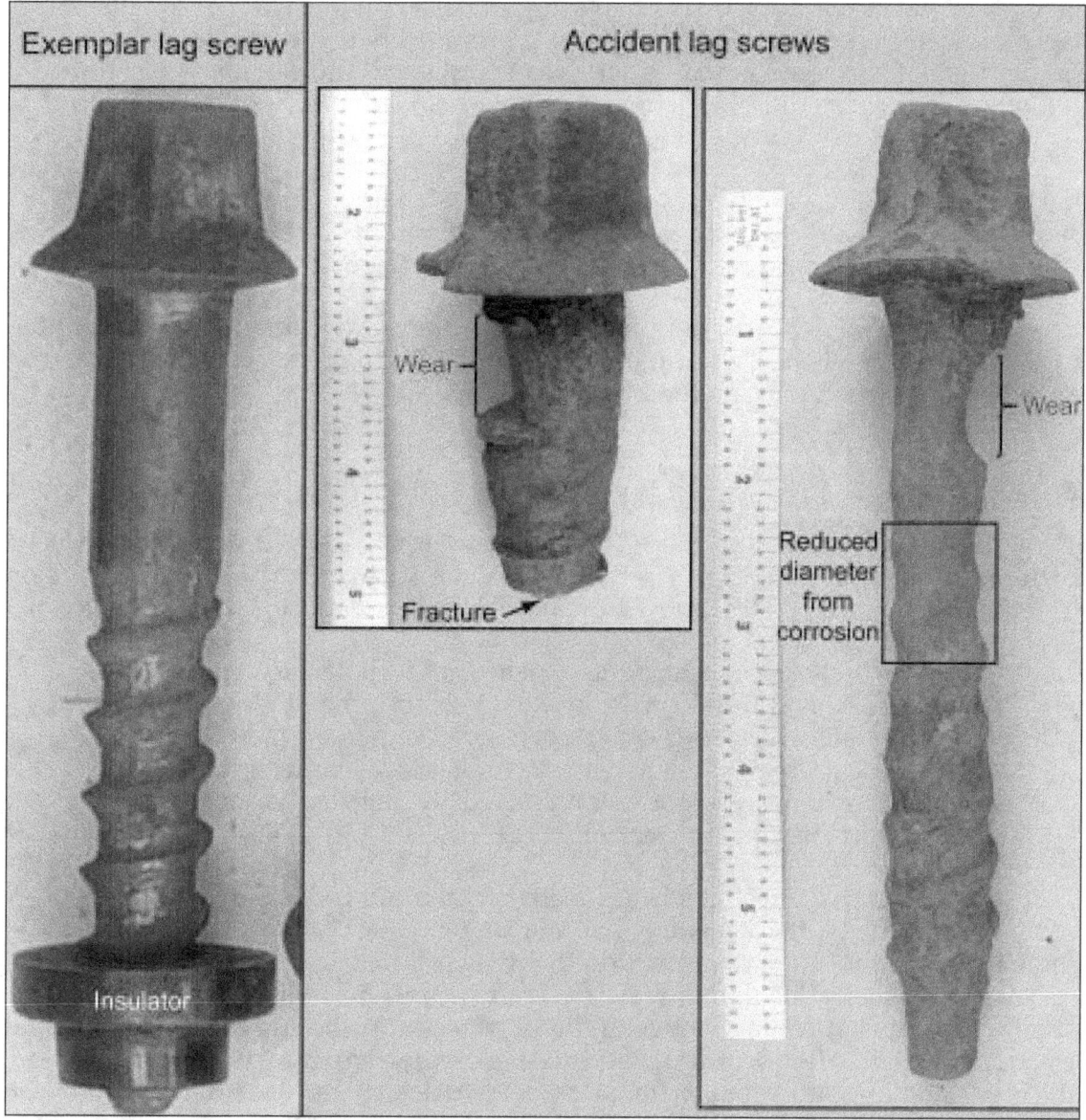

Figure 5. Damaged lag screws from accident location compared to new exemplar lag screw.

Two of the 10 lag screws had fracture surfaces with a light covering of oxides consistent with a recent fracture. The other eight lag screws had fracture surfaces with a significant covering of dark oxides that obliterated the fine features on the surface, and several of these appeared to have been rubbed consistent with preexisting fractures.

Insulator materials between the fasteners and the tie plates were examined. Two types were identified: one was relatively soft and could be easily compressed by hand and the other was relatively hard and firm to the touch. All of the softer insulators were severely worn and missing material on one side. These insulators were typically associated with rail lag screws that had reduced diameters. The harder insulators were associated with lag screws that did not show a significant reduction in diameter in the shank just below the head.

The tie plates examined also showed signs of wear and corrosion. The fastener holes were elongated consistent with contact with the lag screws. One side of each tie plate was thinned from corrosion, and in one tie plate, material was completely missing between one fastener hole and the edge of the tie plate.

The wood tie core samples showed significant amounts of degraded material. Twelve of the 15 samples had portions of the core wood that was soft and crumbled when manipulated by hand.

Steel Corrosion and Electrolysis Effects

On July 24, 2006, the CTA's Engineering Department prepared a memorandum on the subject, "A Prediction of the Rate of Stray Current Corrosion of Rail Fasteners in the Dearborn Subway." The memorandum stated that

> there are two basic mechanisms causing rail fasteners to corrode. The first of these is simple corrosion due to environmental factors, such as water, chlorides, and other corrosive elements that one would normally expect to see whenever steel is placed underground. The second mechanism is corrosion caused by the discharge of direct current directly into an electrolyte (i.e. moist ground).

To reduce the effect of stray current into the rail fastener system, insulators are placed between the fasteners and the tie plates and between the plates and the half-ties. Laboratory examination of the insulators from the derailment area revealed that many insulators were severely worn and missing material on one side, which caused contact between the fasteners and the tie plates and allowed electrical current to flow to ground and accelerate the corrosion process. In addition, the investigation found areas where numerous track spikes were used to maintain gage, which allowed electrical current to flow to ground at the noninsulated spike and accelerate the corrosion process.

Systems

Signal Systems

The Blue Line is equipped with automatic block signals and train stops[34] that govern train movements. Postaccident inspection of the signals and train stops between the Clark/Lake station and the point of derailment revealed no evidence that the train had traveled above posted speeds. The grade timing function for each of the signals between the Clark/Lake station and the derailment site was tested and found to be operating normally. Damage to the signal system adjacent to the derailment was repaired and tested. The signals were found to be operating normally.

Electrical Systems

The derailment area was served by Power Section 307, which is 11,000 feet long. Electricity is provided to this section from the north by the Milwaukee substation and from the south by the East Lake substation. Two breakers, one north of the derailment site and one south, provide electrical protection for this section. Because power is supplied through these two breakers independently, both breakers must open in order to completely remove power from the section. The southern breaker was located about 1,900 feet south of the derailment area and the northern breaker was located about 9,100 feet north of the derailment area. The amount of current drawn through each breaker depends on how close a train is to the breaker.

According to the Supervisory Control and Data Acquisition event log, the southern breaker detected a fault, opened, reset three times, and then opened to lock out as it was designed to do.[35] The northern breaker did not detect the fault, did not open, and had to be manually opened by the power controller. The northern breaker was opened 3 minutes after the southern breaker detected the initial fault. This action removed all power from the third rail in the area of the derailment. However, extensive smoke had been generated by electrical arcing between the third rail and the derailed car at the end of the train.

The breakers used to protect the electrified rail from electrical faults, such as the electrical arcing that occurred as a result of the derailment, can detect faults and open (trip) to stop the electrical current from two types of electrical overloads. One type of overload occurs when the current drawn through the breaker exceeds a specific limit, and another type occurs when the rate of current increase exceeds a specified amount. The breaker south of the arcing event detected the fault through

---

[34] A *train stop* is a mechanical trip arm tied to the signal system that halts the train at a red aspect should the operator fail to do so.

[35] All CTA feeder breakers are designed to detect continuity in the rails for fault conditions prior to closing. The breakers, once tripped, will automatically load measure and reclose if fault conditions exist. If 70 seconds elapse after the initial close command and the breaker has not successfully closed, the breaker will lock out and not reset.

exceeding the current limit, but neither the amount of current nor the rate of current increase was sufficient to cause the breaker north of the arcing to trip. The breakers were originally set to trip when the rate of current increase exceeded 8,000 amperes/second for 200 milliseconds. However, according to the CTA, 4 years before the derailment, it began to reset the breakers to trip at a threshold of 24,000 amperes/second for 100 milliseconds to better distinguish between fluctuations caused by train starts and those caused by remote faults, as well as to increase the reach of the breaker. At the time of the derailment, the closer breaker (the southern breaker) had been modified with the newer settings; however, the more distant breaker (the northern breaker) had not been modified and still had the original settings. The breaker locations and settings prevent unnecessary shutdown of the transit system due to fluctuations of power caused by normal train traffic. Engineering calculations determined that the more distant circuit breaker was too far from the arcing event to cause it to trip from either excessive current or excessive rate of current increase, and even if it had been modified with the new overload settings, the breaker was still too far away from the fault for the arcing event to cause it to trip.

Tunnel Ventilation System

Under normal circumstances, the Blue Line Dearborn Subway tunnels are ventilated by blast shafts and vent shafts. Blast shafts[36] are located outside a subway platform to relieve pressure when trains enter and leave a station. Stations typically have four blast shafts. There are two shafts for each tunnel, which are located at opposite ends of the station. Blast shafts do not have motor operated dampers or fans. Vent shafts are spaced at intervals along each tunnel between stations. Vent shafts do have motor operated dampers and some contain fans. According to the CTA, ventilation during normal operation occurs primarily by the forced ventilation of air caused by the movement of the trains. Differences in temperature and elevation between the subway and the outside can also produce additional ventilation through stack effect.[37]

Emergency ventilation in the Dearborn Subway is handled through various fans. The CTA estimated that the emergency fan system will provide at least four air changes per hour when required. The CTA power controller can remotely control fan operation or other personnel can locally control the fans.[38] When fire, smoke, or fumes are present, CTA's standard practice is to confirm the location of an incident and the circumstances involved before activating ventilation.

At least one vent shaft is located midway between stations along each tunnel. (See figure 6 for the location of the accident in relation to the various fans and stations cited.) The station platform at the Clark/Lake station is equipped

[36] A *blast shaft* is present to relieve air pressure in the tunnel to equalize airflow through the system. A blast shaft is also called a relief shaft.

[37] *Stack effect* is the movement of air resulting from a pressure differential between the outside air and the air inside the tunnel. It is also known as a chimney effect.

[38] Ventilation in the shafts is controlled in order to control temperature through the system.

with an under-platform fan.[39] Farther south from the Clark/Lake station, several dual direction (reversible) fans are located under the continuous[40] platform at the Washington, Monroe, and Jackson stations. Fans north of the accident included fan 133, which was before the Grand/Milwaukee station, and fan 157, which was past the Grand/Milwaukee station.

Fan 108 was closest to the accident location, between the accident and the Clark/Lake station to the south. However, city contractors removed fan 108 during a 2001 renovation project. According to the CTA, this fan has not been replaced due to budget constraints. There are also vent shafts located at the north and south ends of the Clark/Lake station, to which the reversible under-platform fan is connected.

The following time line shows key events after the initial detection of smoke:

At 5:18 p.m., CTA personnel in the northbound tunnel reported (by radio) that smoke was moving toward the Clark/Lake station. In response, the power controller started fan 133 (an exhaust only fan) at this time. By 5:20 p.m., a surveillance camera in the northbound tunnel north of the Clark/Lake station showed smoke moving in the direction of the station. At 5:24 p.m., smoke began to enter the Clark/Lake station side platform area.

At 5:25 p.m., CTA personnel in the northbound tunnel requested that the fan at the Clark/Lake station be turned on in the exhaust mode. The power controller attempted to start fan 157 (an exhaust only fan) in high speed. The fan would not start.[41] The power controller then started the Clark/Lake station under-platform fan in the exhaust mode (direction) at 5:26 p.m., followed by exhaust mode operation of the under-platform fans for the Washington, Monroe, and Jackson stations' continuous platform. The smoke became heavier momentarily at 5:28 p.m., but by 5:35 p.m. it began to clear the Clark/Lake platform.

At 5:37 p.m., CTA personnel reported heavy smoke in the northbound tunnel near fan 133 and that the southbound tunnel was clear. The power controller reported a problem starting fan 157. At 5:47 p.m., smoke increased again at the Clark/Lake platform. At 5:51 p.m., CTA personnel in the northbound tunnel reported heavy smoke in the location of the vent shaft for fan 108 and directed the power controller to put the under-platform fan at Clark/Lake and the continuous platform fans for the Washington, Monroe, and Jackson stations in the supply mode.

---

[39] *Under-platform fans* assist with ventilation control within the station.

[40] One platform serves all three stations.

[41] When the fan was tested later, it started normally.

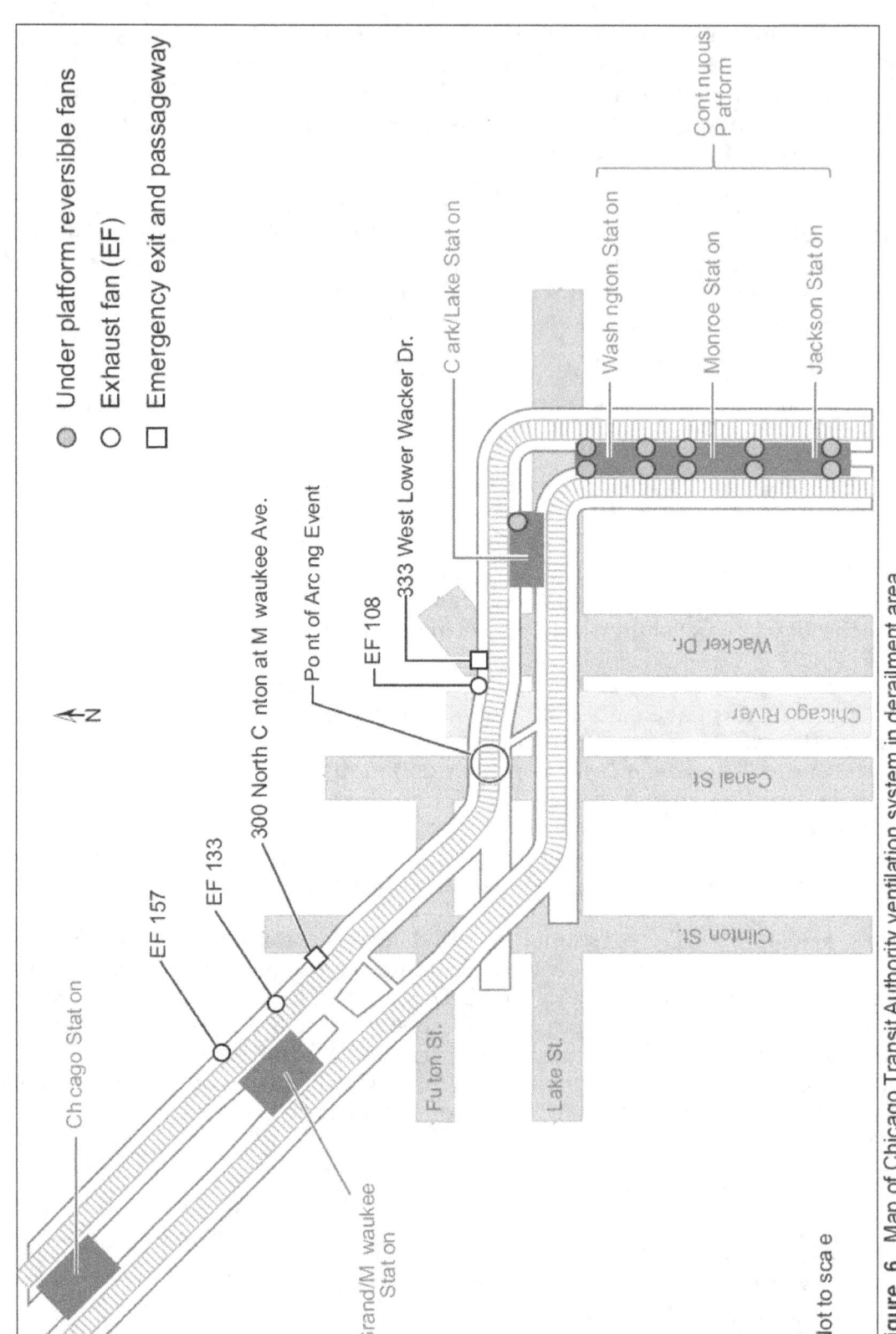

Figure 6. Map of Chicago Transit Authority ventilation system in derailment area.

Under platform reversible fans

Exhaust fan (EF)

Emergency exit and passageway

Chicago Station

EF 157

EF 133

300 North Clinton at Milwaukee Ave.

Grand/Milwaukee Station

Point of Arcing Event

333 West Lower Wacker Dr.

EF 108

Clark/Lake Station

Washington Station

Monroe Station

Jackson Station

Continuous Platform

Fulton St.

Lake St.

Clinton St.

Chicago River

Wacker Dr.

Not to scale

The power controller stopped the exhaust operation of the Clark/Lake under-platform fan and then immediately turned this fan on the high setting in the supply mode. At 5:52 p.m., the power controller stopped the exhaust operation of the under-platform fans for the Washington, Monroe, and Jackson stations' continuous platform. At 5:56 p.m., the power controller turned these fans back on the high setting in the supply mode. The Clark/Lake platform was cleared of smoke by 6:00 p.m.

Government Oversight of Safety

In 1991, the Safety Board conducted a safety study[42] that addressed the safety oversight of rail rapid transit systems. On December 18, 1991, considering the Board's safety recommendations and studies, Congress enacted the Intermodal Surface Transportation Efficiency Act of 1991 (Public Law 102-240), which added Section 289 to the Federal Transit Act. This required that those States that have a fixed-guideway system (such as CTA's), which is not regulated by the Federal Railroad Administration, to designate a State agency to oversee the safety of the guideway system. It also authorized the Federal Transit Administration (FTA) to withhold some transit funding should a State fail to implement a safety program.

In 49 CFR Part 659, the FTA requires each State to designate an oversight agency to conduct safety and security oversight of its rail transit system. In Illinois, that agency is the Regional Transportation Authority (RTA). The State agency (RTA) requires the transit agency (CTA) to develop a system safety program plan that includes elements identified by the FTA, and the State agency reviews the transit agency's compliance with the system safety program plan and its implementation of corrective actions to address safety deficiencies. At least every 3 years, the oversight agency must conduct an on-site review of the rail transit agency's implementation of its system safety program plan and system security plan, and prepare and issue a report (triennial report) containing findings and recommendations resulting from that review.

The FTA requires that system safety program plans include operating and maintenance rules and procedures to address safety related infrastructure such as track, including track inspections and maintenance. The rail transit agency must provide the State oversight agency with verification that the corrective action has been implemented or that a corrective action plan has been prepared to address findings from safety reviews. The State oversight agency must monitor the implementation of each approved corrective action plan.

With the events of September 11, 2001, the FTA temporarily ceased conducting audits of State system safety oversight programs in order to divert resources to address security assessments and evaluations at rail transit agencies.

---

[42] National Transportation Safety Board, *Oversight of Rail Rapid Transit Safety*, Railroad Safety Study NTSB/SS-91/02 (Washington, DC: NTSB, 1991).

The FTA resumed conducting audits of State safety oversight programs in 2005 and expects to complete audits on all rail transit systems by September 2009.[43] The FTA's last audit of RTA's State system safety oversight program was conducted in 2000, and the audit report did not refer to any track related safety problems.

Within a 2-month period in 2001, the CTA experienced two similar rear-end collisions involving CTA rapid transit trains. Both accidents were preceded by the train operators' failure to comply with operating rules designed to prevent collisions. The Safety Board's special investigation[44] of these two accidents highlighted deficiencies in CTA management's approach to ensuring rules compliance among its operators. As a result of this special investigation, the Safety Board issued Safety Recommendation R-02-18[45] to the FTA.

On April 29, 2005, the FTA published a revised rule for 49 CFR Part 659 in the *Federal Register*. The rule removed the reference to the *American Public Transportation Association (APTA) Manual* and added equivalent requirements to Part 659.15 "State Safety Program Standard." The implementation of the FTA's final rule constituted an acceptable alternate approach to the Board's recommendation, and Safety Recommendation R-02-18 was classified "Closed — Acceptable Alternate Action" on June 21, 2005.

Another change implemented in the April 29, 2005, rulemaking was specific language in 49 CFR 659.39(c)(2), "Oversight Agency Reporting to the Federal Transit Administration," requiring the State safety oversight agency to submit "a report documenting and tracking findings from three-year safety review activities, and whether a three-year safety review has been completed since the last annual report was submitted." Prior to this rule change, FTA regulations did not specifically require the results of triennial safety review reports and the FTA would not necessarily have been aware of them unless it had conducted an audit.

The FTA has identified its "Top 10 Safety Action Priorities" as part of its Rail Transit Safety Action Plan. These priorities include "Improving Compliance with Operating and Maintenance Rules." On May 8, 2007, the FTA issued a letter (see appendix B) outlining new initiatives it is taking to address track worker protection and maintenance oversight issues. Among these initiatives are rail transit workshops on maintenance oversight and track inspection training. The FTA reports that it will continue its partnership with APTA in the Rail Transit Standards Program to identify and address issues raised as a result of the workshops and track inspection training. The FTA also plans to develop a track inspection

---

[43] FTA estimates that the RTA program will be audited in 2008.

[44] National Transportation Safety Board, *Two Rear-End Collisions Involving Chicago Transit Authority Rapid Transit Trains at Chicago, Illinois, June 17 and August 3, 2001*, Special Investigation Report NTSB/SIR-02/01 (Washington, DC: NTSB, 2002).

[45] To the FTA: "Adopt the American Public Transportation Association manual that contains updated language on auditing the effectiveness of operating rules compliance programs, and simultaneously modify 49 *Code of Federal Regulations* Part 659 so that the Part always references the current American Public Transportation Association manual."

training course specifically for track inspectors and supervisors to address the unique demands of track inspection in the rail transit environment. The course will initially be offered at the Nation's 13 heavy rail transit agencies and over time be expanded to commuter rail agencies and light rail agencies.

RTA Inspection

The RTA's core missions are financial oversight and regional planning. It is guided by a 13-member Board of Directors, and it employs a professional staff of approximately 80 people led by an Executive Director. The RTA said that two employees spend about 25 percent of their time on the CTA safety oversight program. Each has attended specific safety training provided by the U.S. Department of Transportation's Transportation Safety Institute.

The RTA's Rail Safety Oversight Program includes reviewing major accident investigations conducted by outside agencies, conducting on-site triennial reviews, reviewing CTA's hazard management plans, preparing FTA reports, and reviewing CTA's annual internal safety audit. The RTA manager for this program stated that while his office meets requirements established by the FTA, the RTA's role is to oversee the CTA's safety program. He also stated that the State of Illinois act authorizing this safety oversight program does not provide regulatory authority.

The RTA contracted with Battelle Memorial Institute to provide rail safety oversight consultant services, including accident investigations and on-site safety reviews. An RTA Triennial On-Site Safety Review of the CTA rail system was conducted in August 2004 by its contractor. The RTA review was conducted between August 2 and 13, 2004, with the final report released January 21, 2005, and revised/updated in coordination with the CTA on September 27, 2005. The RTA's report on this review addressed all aspects of the CTA's System Safety Program Plan. The report included five findings in the "Track Structures and Maintenance" section. Each finding was followed by additional comments or observations. The RTA considered these observations to be separate from the findings, requiring no corrective actions.

The first finding stated that "The CTA Track Department is very attentive to field conditions and maintenance issues, and seems to have a solid program for identifying track issues during inspections." However, after the finding, the report stated that the CTA track inspection personnel levels are lean as compared to other similar transit systems.

The second finding stated that "The Track Department is taking delivery on some important track maintenance equipment; this equipment will help to improve track conditions and supplement inspection activities." After the finding, the report stated that during the last triennial review in 2001 there was a lack of surfacing equipment[46] that made general track geometry repairs difficult.

---

[46] The CTA did take delivery of a tamping machine and ballast stabilizer in 2005.

The third finding stated that "Track inspection training should be guided by a course/career outline or similar document to ensure continuity and repeatability." However, after the finding, the report also stated that the on-the-job-training may not be uniform and equal and that the CTA may wish to designate practical tests and field exercises that the student must complete.

The fourth finding stated that "There is currently no rail testing for track geometry or internal rail defects (ultrasonic testing)." After the finding, the report stated that nearly every rail transit system in the United States performs track geometry and internal rail defect testing, and both types of testing provide important backups to visual inspections and detect track flaws in areas that are normally imperceptible to track personnel.

The fifth finding stated that "Track inspection documentation is relatively simple yet effective; a few small record-keeping areas could be improved." However, after the finding, the report stated that conditions in the State (Red) and Dearborn (Blue) Subway tunnels included a number of areas (often where gage problems exist) where track plates were visibly skewed and/or twisted. The report further stated that "This would seem to indicate that they and their fasteners are probably ineffective." There were problems with the deteriorated half-ties and certain areas had mud and excessive water on the track structure. Another comment identified a large number of gage rods on the Red Line and suggested that although gage rods are necessary for temporary or emergency repairs, the number of them indicates that there are large-scale track gage issues in that area.

In response to the RTA's triennial review, the CTA noted that the first, second, and fifth findings required no action.

In response to the third finding, the CTA said that it was revising its track training handbook and researching continuing education courses for inspectors. However, CTA training personnel said after the accident that none of these corrective actions had been implemented. Further, their training modules did not specifically address tunnel inspections and maintenance. The CTA's Manager of Track had reviewed the triennial review report and stated that the CTA was aware of the observations listed after the findings. When asked if any specific followups were prompted as a result of the observations listed after the fifth finding, he stated that the roadmasters were aware of the information in the observations and had been taking actions as deemed necessary to take care of problem areas.

In response to the fourth finding, the CTA said that its track department would continue to explore on-track rail testing and would seek funding to implement it. The CTA said that it also had reached out to other transit agencies around the country to explore alternatives and best practices and that it would complete planning for track geometry testing with prospective contractors by December 31, 2006. Because of the derailment, the CTA requested additional funding and, therefore, was able to complete the track geometry testing in October 2006.

The RTA accepted the corrective action plans presented to it by the CTA as a result of the Triennial On-Site Safety Review. When asked why the RTA did not follow up on the observations noted in the triennial review, such as the visibly skewed or twisted track plates and deteriorated half-ties in the Dearborn Subway tunnel, an RTA representative said that it only follows up on findings. The RTA representative said that the RTA considered these observations to be comments and not findings in the System Safety Program Plan. In accordance with the RTA's *System Safety Program Standard and Procedures*,[47] had the RTA treated these comments as findings and determined that actions should be taken to correct the deficiencies, the RTA should have required the CTA to prepare corrective action plans for those items. Such plans must include identification of the deficiency, the actions necessary to address it, a schedule for implementation, identification of the individuals responsible to take these actions, and the costs involved. A corrective action plan must be approved by the RTA for each deficiency. If the RTA rejects the CTA's plans, then the CTA must submit revised plans. According to the RTA's *System Safety Program Standard and Procedures*,

> The objective of this procedure, adopted to comply with 49 CFR Part 659, Subpart C, § 659.37, is to ensure that corrective action plans are developed and implemented for deficiencies identified as a result of the safety oversight program.

According to the FTA, the FTA did not conduct an audit of the RTA, nor did the FTA receive a copy of the RTA's 2005 triennial report.

American Public Transportation Association Guidance

APTA provides guidance to assist its members in developing minimum requirements for inspecting and maintaining rail transit system tracks. Examples of APTA guidance in the "Standard for Rail Transit Track Inspection and Maintenance"[48] include rail fastener requirements, replacement of corroded rail, keeping drains free of debris to accommodate water flow, and minimum qualifications[49] for track inspectors. The guidance also states that both internal rail defect detection and automated track geometry inspection shall be conducted annually.

---

[47] *The Regional Transportation Authority's System Safety Program Standard and Procedures For Overseeing The Chicago Transit Authority's Rail Fixed Guideway System*, August 2006 Update.

[48] The American Public Transportation Association, Section 2 in *Volume 5—Fixed Structures*, APTA RT-S-FS-002-02 (APTA, Washington, DC: 2004).

[49] The qualified person should have at least 2 years of experience in inspecting track, constructing or maintaining track, or special track work; or a combination of track maintenance experience and training in track inspection; or have progressive satisfactory supervisory experience on another transit or railroad system. In addition, the qualified person has to be able to demonstrate knowledge and understanding of the track standards, be able to detect deviations from the standards, and be able to prescribe appropriate remedial actions for the detected deviations.

The CTA requested and received an APTA safety audit in 2004. These audits, which are provided as a service to APTA members, cover all elements of the system safety program plan. Regarding track and facilities issues, the audit noted that track geometry vehicle inspections were needed, that standard on-track vehicles would not meet CTA clearance requirements, and that the CTA was seeking sources of funding for this project. The audit also noted that System Safety and Facility Maintenance personnel must meet specific training and education requirements.

Postaccident Actions

The CTA has advised the Safety Board of organizational changes and other actions it has taken that address track maintenance and inspection processes and training, including the following:

- The CTA completed a detailed track inspection of the Blue Line Subway, including the derailment area, and all corroded tie plates, lag screws, and rail clips have been replaced.

- A contractor was hired to replace and upgrade all light fixtures in the Dearborn, State, and Kimball Subway tunnels. The CTA expects this work to be completed by December 2007.

- The CTA contracted with an outside firm to perform track strength and track geometry measurements throughout the entire rail system. Those tests were completed in October 2006[50] and will be conducted on an annual basis.

- The CTA has completed a reorganization of the engineering and maintenance departments and has separated track inspection activities from track maintenance activities. Thirty-six positions were added to the 69 inspector/maintenance positions, resulting in a new total of 105 positions. Forty-two positions are dedicated to track inspections 5 days per week, and 63 positions are dedicated to performing track maintenance.

- All track inspectors were required to undergo 3 days of refresher training, and this will be conducted on an annual basis.

- Track maintenance standards have been revised to reduce the likelihood of corrosion. The new standards require that when rail is replaced, a new insulated fastener system will be installed in conjunction with the rail replacement.

- All safety officers and system safety engineers have completed a track standards class and a track inspection class. They are now conducting monthly reviews of the track inspection reports.

---

[50] Several areas of poor gage were detected that resulted in either repairs being made or slow zones being placed in effect.

- On a monthly interval, System Safety personnel are accompanying track inspectors on an inspection.

- System Safety personnel are providing feedback to track maintenance personnel on any irregularities they observe during inspections or reviews.

The CTA provided longer-term action plans to make repairs and to improve the inspection process. Those items are as follows:

- The CTA plans to develop a new computerized database with handheld units for field employees to integrate maintenance records and other information to more effectively and economically maintain all tracks. The CTA took delivery of 32 handheld units and is evaluating their functionality and use in a pilot program.

- A contract is in place to replace 4,000 rail half-ties in the Blue Line Subway. An additional 1,200 half-ties have been added to the contract, and this work is scheduled to be completed by the end of September 2007. Initially, 4,000 half-ties were scheduled for replacement in the Red Line Subway and an additional 4,500 half-ties have been added for replacement. This work is also scheduled for completion by the end of 2007. The area of the derailment has had larger tie plates and new fasteners installed; however, the half-ties were not replaced.

- In November 2006, the CTA began working to grout all areas of water seepage in the subway, and the work is continuing as seepage areas are identified.

In the August 17, 2006, *Ventilation Performance Report*, the CTA reviewed the problems it had experienced trying to identify the location of the derailed train and evacuate its tunnel system. The CTA has a train indication system that alerts personnel in the control center to the location of a train. Prior to the accident, the train indication system had already been installed in the State Street, Dan Ryan, and O'Hare Subways, and the CTA expects to install it in the Dearborn Subway by 2009. The CTA has installed reflective station signs displaying the track station number every 100 feet on the tunnel walls. The Dearborn Subway signs are 95 percent installed, and the CTA expects to have completed a quality control check of all the station signs by the end of 2007. As of March 2007, the CTA distributed revised emergency response maps that reflect the locations of all emergency call boxes and their identification numbers.

The CTA's *Ventilation Performance Report* included the following recommendations for improving the tunnel ventilation system:

- Replace all fans in the Dearborn, State, Kimball, and O'Hare Subways, including fan 108.

- Require that all new fans placed in the system be reversible.
- Program smoke control matrices into the fan controls that indicate which fans should be on supply and which fans should be on exhaust during a fire/smoke incident.

The CTA reported that funding is not available for the above proposed fan improvements. The CTA has updated the fan labeling in the control center to ensure that operators are aware of the direction of airflow for all fans.

ANALYSIS

Exclusions

The operator of Chicago Transit Authority (CTA) train number 220 was qualified for his operational responsibilities, rested, and familiar with the territory. The operator and witnesses stated that there were no abnormalities in train handling prior to the derailment. Postaccident inspection of the signals and train stops between the Clark/Lake station and the point of derailment revealed no evidence of excessive speed. Federally required postaccident drug and alcohol testing was negative for the operator. The Safety Board concludes that the following were not factors in the accident: the operator's qualifications, his operation of the train, or drug or alcohol use.

A review of the preaccident mechanical inspections and repairs for each railcar did not reveal anything unusual. Postaccident mechanical testing of the equipment was also unremarkable. Each component and car performed as intended. The derailed car was examined in detail and showed no signs of preaccident distress. Further, the track structure that the train traversed before it reached the point of derailment showed no evidence that a distressed wheel had applied an abnormal load. The base of the rail exhibited corrosion in some areas, and the wear pattern concludes that there was no preaccident mechanical or component failure on any of the train's cars.

The Accident

The northbound CTA train number 220 was proceeding normally in a 2° left-hand curve just north of the Clark/Lake station when a blue light alarm indicated a problem as the last car derailed. Postaccident track gage measurements and wheel mark evidence revealed that the left wheel from the last car of the train had dropped from the inner rail of the curve into the gage of the track at CTA station 106+53.

Examination of the derailment site revealed that multiple rail fastener devices (lag screws, rail clip assemblies, and tie plates) for the outer rail in the curve at this location had been corroded, worn, bent, broken, and/or displaced from their associated half-ties, and the rail had moved laterally outward under load. The base of the rail exhibited corrosion in some areas, and the wear pattern on the inner rail of the curve exhibited dark streaks that extended from the center of the railhead outward to the field side (outside) of the railhead surface. This type of dark area indicates that wide gage was present because the wheels were not in full contact with the railhead. The CTA track inspectors responsible for inspecting this area where the derailment occurred had not recorded these wide **gage indica**tions. Also, gage measurements on the track near the derailment, but unaffected by the forces of it, showed that the gage was wider than what was allowable for the track speed. In fact, one area of the gage had exceeded 58 inches and, according to CTA Requirement 301, should have been placed out of service.

Abrasion on the tie plates and ties in the area of the derailment showed that before the accident, the rail had been moving laterally as trains passed over that section of the track. Laboratory examination of the broken or displaced rail lag screws and tie plates revealed significant corrosion. Rubbing of the fracture faces indicated that several lag screws had failed sometime prior to the derailment. Many lag screws showed severe wear in areas where they had contact with the tie plates, and tie plate holes for the fasteners were elongated. In addition, the core samples from the wood half-ties revealed that the wood had degraded and was too soft to adequately hold the lag screws. The CTA's Engineering Department identified two corrosion mechanisms: corrosion caused by environmental factors, such as water and chlorides found in the track bed, and corrosion caused by the discharge of stray direct current going to ground.

The train stops on each car and the test data from the signal system indicate that the train was traveling at or below the posted speed limit of 25 mph, and excess speed was not a factor. The evidence indicates that lateral forces generated as the accident train moved through the curve forced the outer curve rail outward and fractured or bent the few remaining intact lag screws. The Safety Board concludes that the tie plates and fastener system failed to maintain the track gage because of the effects of corrosion and/or wear on the rails and rail fastener system, and degraded half-ties.

CTA Track Inspections

The corrosion and/or wear found on the rails and the fastener system and the degraded (rotten) wood in the half-ties occurred over a long period of time. The investigation focused on why these problems were not identified and repaired before the derailment. Factors examined in detail included the general condition of the system, the inspection environment, the length of territories, training, and oversight.

Condition of the System

The CTA Blue Line was placed into service about 55 years before the derailment, and many of the track components had not been replaced since then. The CTA was aware of the corrosion and wear problems and the degraded half-ties. There was evidence that some maintenance repairs had been performed by the track inspectors north and south of the derailment, but not specifically in the area of the derailment. According to the CTA, the priorities for track maintenance on the Dearborn Subway are to replace the wood half-ties with concrete slabs and replace the rail as necessary, and these maintenance repairs were made about 1 mile north of the point of derailment. The CTA reports that since the accident larger tie plates and new fasteners have been installed in the area of the derailment; however, no further track work is scheduled. Therefore, the Safety Board believes that the RTA should determine if track safety deficiencies on the CTA's Dearborn Subway in the area of the derailment have been adequately repaired.

Environment and Length of Territory

A postaccident walking inspection of the territory that included the area of the derailment found that the inspection conditions within the tunnel were not ideal. The tunnel lighting was limited,[51] standing water covered areas of the tunnel floor, and mud and debris covered drainage areas. Also, a train came every 7 minutes, and the track inspectors had to step over the exposed 600-volt third rail and stand against the tunnel wall until it passed. Despite these limitations, there was ample evidence of track problems. The Safety Board concludes that the dark area on the inner rail of the curve, the abrasion on the tie plates and ties, the broken lag screws, the tie plates' elongated fastener holes, and poor drainage in the area of the derailment were all readily observable and should have been documented during walking inspections.

The section roadmaster for the area of the derailment stated that he did not have any backup inspectors to cover a territory when an inspector was absent. He said that inspections were halted when a priority maintenance situation occurred, and he used a group of his inspectors to make the necessary repairs. The investigation also revealed that hundreds of inspection records were missing, which further indicates that critical track inspections were not being performed.

The review of the amount of time available to conduct the inspection, the distance of track to be inspected, and the train density revealed that the track inspectors could not complete an inspection of the entire 6.22-mile territory during the 9:00 a.m. to 3:00 p.m. timeframe allotted for the inspection. The review of the inspection records for the accident area and other track territories on the CTA system found that routine inspection reports often had multiple track defects concentrated in certain areas while no defects were noted in the remainder of the territory. This uneven distribution of defects further indicates that track inspectors did not complete their inspections during the allotted hours. The Safety Board concludes that track inspectors in the Dearborn Subway did not have sufficient time allotted for inspecting all of their assigned territory twice a week as prescribed. Therefore, the Safety Board believes that the CTA should evaluate all territories to determine the number of inspectors and the amount of time needed to ensure that adequate track inspections are conducted, and implement appropriate changes.

---

[51] Since the accident, the CTA has reported that subway lighting is being upgraded in multiple tunnels including the Dearborn Subway tunnels.

Qualifications and Training

The track problems in this accident were evident and should have been identified. This prompted a review of the CTA track inspector training and qualifications as compared to other rail passenger programs in the industry. A survey of several transit agencies and passenger railroads revealed that the CTA had the lowest experience and training requirements for its track inspectors. The CTA can select track maintenance workers to become inspectors after only 1 year of track experience. Also, a prospective inspector may have little real track maintenance experience or knowledge. In comparison, the surveyed agencies and railroads have an application process, and only the most qualified senior track workers or foremen are selected to be track inspectors.

The CTA's General Manager of Power and Way Maintenance stated that he believed that a track inspector's position requires more experience and comprehensive training than it is currently given and that the track inspector's status should be higher than that of maintenance workers and laborers. He compared the position to that of CTA's signal inspectors, who are required to complete apprenticeships before being considered for those positions.

The CTA's 1 day of classroom training in track inspection that was in place before the accident was the least amount of classroom training required by the transit agencies and/or railroads surveyed. The other agencies and railroads not only select experienced personnel, but also they typically require from 1 to 4 weeks of training in track inspection and have recurrent training thereafter to ensure that their employees maintain continued competency in critical areas.

The CTA 1-day classroom training covered the CTA's *Track Maintenance Standards Manual*. This manual listed 16 possible indications of a gage problem including dark streaks on the inside rail of a curve, lateral movement of tie plate on the tie or rail on the tie plate, missing spikes, and poor tie conditions. Most of these conditions were observed during the postaccident inspections of the derailment area. However, as one CTA track inspector pointed out, the class covered too much information in too short a time.

The CTA's classroom training also did not cover conditions found in tunnels or on elevated structures. Unique conditions, such as standing water, electrolysis, and darkness that requires working by flashlight, can occur in tunnels. These conditions can cause track problems to differ depending on the environment and the construction, and track inspection methods may therefore vary depending on the visibility and the location of the track. The Safety Board concludes that the CTA track inspection training program did not adequately prepare inspectors to perform their required duties and it did not address the unique demands of inspecting and maintaining elevated track structures or track structures located inside tunnels. Since the accident, the CTA has informed the Board that it has lengthened its track training program and now mandates track refresher training on an annual basis. It also is developing a new comprehensive track inspection training program to be completed by 2008. The Federal Transit Administration (FTA) has recognized that most transit agencies need assistance with track inspection and maintenance programs, and it is developing a program that includes workshops as well as classroom training to address this need. Although the CTA has taken action to improve its track inspector training program, the FTA is developing a course for all transit agencies' track inspector programs that would likely enhance the CTA's efforts. The Safety Board believes that the FTA should schedule the CTA as a priority for receiving the maintenance oversight workshop and the training course to be developed for track inspectors and supervisors that will address the unique demands of track inspection in the rail transit environment. The Safety Board also believes that the CTA should schedule as a priority the maintenance oversight workshop and the training course that the FTA plans to develop for track inspectors and supervisors that will address the unique demands of track inspection in the rail transit environment.

Other Track Inspection Methods

The limited lighting conditions and high train frequency in the subway systems made it difficult for inspectors to detect evidence of track problems. Also, some of the corrosion and fractures on the lag screws involved in the derailment would not have been readily observable because some of the damage was below the tie plates. Most U.S. railroads and transit agencies supplement the ability of their track inspectors to identify track problems by performing periodic inspections of the track using track geometry strength and condition test vehicles. These vehicles can detect track gage problems that are not readily observable by a track inspector. The vehicles also measure the track gage under load. The CTA used a track geometry vehicle to inspect all of its mainline track in October 2006. As a result, several areas of poor gage were detected that resulted in either repairs being made or slow zones being placed in effect. The Safety Board concludes that the use of a track geometry strength and condition test vehicle would have simulated train loads and better identified areas of poor track gage and the need for corrective action.

Many potentially dangerous internal rail defects have no external indications and can only be detected through other means (for example, ultrasonic testing). Therefore, U.S. railroads and transit agencies periodically use automated equipment on their tracks to perform a continuous search along the entire rail length for internal defects. The RTA Triennial On-Site Safety Review report stated that the CTA had "no rail testing for track geometry or internal rail defects (ultrasonic testing)." Both types of testing provide important backups to visual inspections and detect track flaws in areas that are normally imperceptible to track personnel. The CTA has informed the Safety Board that it is procuring contracts for annual track geometry and ultrasonic testing that will be in place and in use by the end of 2007. However, the regular use of track geometry vehicles and periodic inspection of rail for internal defects has not been incorporated into the CTA's System Safety

Program Plan, which would help to ensure continued use as part of a long-term program. The American Public Transportation Association's (APTA's) standard for transit track inspection and maintenance recommends the annual use of track geometry cars and ultrasonic inspection of rails. The standard also addresses other actions needed to address many of the safety deficiencies listed in the RTA's safety review. Therefore, the Safety Board believes that the CTA should, as part of the effort to improve its track safety program, examine all of the elements in APTA's "Standard for Rail Transit Track Inspection and Maintenance" and incorporate all appropriate elements of this standard in its system safety program. Specifically, the CTA should include the regular use of track geometry vehicle inspections and the inspection of rail for internal defects in its system safety program.

CTA Oversight

Direct supervision of the CTA track inspectors is provided by the section roadmasters. A section roadmaster is responsible for a given territory and several track inspection teams. Although the section roadmaster for the derailment area communicated with his track inspectors by phone or radio throughout the day, he did not often review the quality and completeness of their work. In fact, he stated that during the 5 months prior to the accident, he had only performed the required monthly inspection once.

The investigation revealed hundreds of missing or incomplete track inspection records. It also revealed records that showed track defects without parallel records showing that repairs were made. The lack of critical records and the poor preparation of those that did exist indicate that some roadmasters were not reviewing the records in accordance with CTA requirements. The CTA's Track Engineer IV Maintenance and the Manager of Track stated that they were unaware of this problem and they relied on the roadmasters to review the records.

The CTA utilized a System Safety Program Plan approach to monitor and inspect the varying functions within its departments, including the track department. System Safety personnel were responsible for reviewing the track inspection and maintenance program. However, they did not monitor the inspection of the track structure or check the inspection records for completeness, nor did they have the technical track expertise to perform those functions. The System Safety personnel stated that they primarily concentrated on the walkway areas in the tunnels and the emergency exits, and they left the oversight of track inspection to the track department. In fact, the 2005 annual internal safety audit did not identify any problems with the track or inspection records.

Overall, a deficient safety culture existed at the CTA that allowed the track infrastructure to deteriorate to an unsafe condition. Industry standards for inspecting and testing the track were not incorporated into CTA practices. Inspection records across the system were either missing or incomplete. Training and qualification requirements for track inspectors were less than those of other rail passenger carriers. There was a lack of effective supervisory oversight. The System Safety program failed to identify track program deficiencies. Further, when an outside review raised questions about deficient track conditions and the number of track inspection and maintenance employees available to do the work as compared to other similar operations within the industry, the CTA did not take corrective action to address the issues. The investigation found a series of latent conditions and active failures at many levels throughout the CTA corporate structure, which is characteristic of an organizational accident.[52] The Safety Board concludes that because the CTA failed to establish an effective track inspection and maintenance program, unsafe track conditions and deficiencies were not corrected. Since the accident, the CTA has informed the Board that it has significantly increased staff in the track inspection and maintenance areas and reorganized its engineering and maintenance departments to separate track inspection activities from track maintenance activities. Thirty-six positions were added to the 69 inspector/ maintenance positions, resulting in a new total of 105 positions. Although the Board notes that the CTA is making improvements, the Board remains concerned about the CTA's failure to recognize and correct unsafe track conditions identified by the RTA before the accident. Therefore, the Safety Board believes that the CTA should correct all safety deficiencies identified by the RTA in its most recent and future safety inspections and reviews, regardless of whether those deficiencies are labeled as "findings," "observations," or some other term. Further, because the Chicago Transit Board governs and administers the CTA and is responsible for overseeing transit facility operations, the Safety Board believes that the Chicago Transit Board should direct the CTA to correct all safety deficiencies identified by the RTA in its most recent and future safety inspections and reviews, regardless of whether those deficiencies are labeled as "findings," "observations," or some other term.

Government Oversight

The State of Illinois' Regional Transportation Authority (RTA) hired a contractor to conduct the Triennial On-Site Safety Review of the CTA's System Safety Program Plan. The report from the triennial review performed in 2004 listed numerous track maintenance and inspection safety issues that did not prompt any corrective actions, including the following: skewed or twisted track plates (on the Dearborn Subway) indicating ineffective fasteners that often indicate the existence of wide gage problems; deteriorated half-ties and areas of mud and excessive water on the track structure on the Red and Blue lines; a large number of gage rods indicating large-scale track issues on the Red line; lean levels of track inspection personnel as compared to other similar transit systems; and inadequate training of track inspection personnel.

---

[52] Dr. James Reason states that "organizational accidents have multiple causes involving many people operating at different levels of their respective companies." J. Reason, *Managing the Risks of Organizational Accidents* (Burlington: Ashgate Publishing Company, 1997) 1.

The CTA was aware of these track maintenance and inspection deficiencies; however, most of the track deficiencies identified in the triennial review were still present when the accident occurred about 18 months after the final report was issued. The Safety Board is concerned that when asked why the RTA did not follow up on all the track safety issues identified in the triennial review, the RTA representative said that the RTA only follows up on findings in the triennial review and it did not consider these observations to be findings that would warrant further action.

Although the system safety reviews were an important step in identifying dangerous conditions on the CTA transit system, the RTA did not fully utilize its oversight authority. The RTA did not require the CTA to prepare corrective action plans to address all safety conditions identified in its review. Further, the RTA report highlighted positive findings that were inconsistent with the additional observations of serious safety conditions. The Safety Board concludes that because the RTA failed to follow up with the CTA and prompt action to correct safety deficiencies identified in the triennial report, unsafe track conditions continued to exist that should have been corrected. Therefore, the Safety Board believes that the RTA should strengthen its followup action on CTA system safety reviews to ensure that the CTA corrects all identified safety deficiencies, regardless of whether those deficiencies are labeled as "findings," "observations," or some other term. Further, the Safety Board believes that the State of Illinois should evaluate the RTA's effectiveness, procedures, and authority, and take action to ensure that all safety deficiencies identified during rail transit safety inspections and reviews of the CTA are corrected, regardless of whether those deficiencies are labeled as "findings," "observations," or some other term.

The FTA's transit oversight program requires that FTA inspectors perform an on-site audit of each State's system safety oversight program every 3 years. Prior to the accident, the FTA's last audit of the RTA program was conducted in 2000. With the events of September 11, 2001, the FTA temporarily ceased conducting State system safety oversight program audits and focused its resources on security assessments and evaluations at rail transit agencies. During this period, the FTA revised 49 *Code of Federal Regulations* (CFR) Part 659 and required additional safety and security measures to be taken by transit agencies. The FTA has now resumed its on-site audits of each State's system safety oversight program, and the RTA is scheduled to be audited in 2008.

The FTA did not receive a copy of the RTA's January 2005 Triennial On-Site Safety Review report that identified numerous track maintenance and inspection safety deficiencies. Although the FTA did not review this report, in April 2005 the FTA did revise 49 CFR Part 659 to require State safety oversight agencies to provide in their annual submissions (by March 15 of each year) a report documenting and tracking findings from 3-year (triennial) safety review activities. This provides another opportunity at the Federal level to ensure rail transit agencies are providing effective safety oversight. However, the Safety Board is concerned that observations or other comments relating to safety deficiencies might not be included in these annual submissions unless they are labeled as a finding in the triennial safety report. The Safety Board concludes that the FTA's oversight of the RTA's Rail Safety Oversight Program was inadequate and failed to prompt actions needed to correct track safety deficiencies on the CTA's rail transit system. Therefore, the Safety Board believes that the FTA should modify its program to ensure that State safety oversight agencies take action to prompt rail transit agencies to correct all safety deficiencies that are identified as a result of oversight inspections and safety reviews, regardless of whether those deficiencies are labeled as "findings," "observations," or some other term.

A 2006 U.S. Government Accountability Office report[53] on the FTA State Safety Oversight program also recognized that the FTA had failed to keep to its stated 3-year audit schedule of the State safety oversight agencies in the years after September 11, 2001. The report determined that this failure resulted in a lack of information to track program trends and made it difficult for FTA officials to develop performance measures and goals to enhance its System Safety Oversight program. The report also recognized that the FTA faces some challenges in managing and implementing its program because officials interviewed from 16 of the 24 State system safety oversight agencies said that they do not have enough qualified staff to manage their programs. Also, officials interviewed from both transit and oversight agencies stated that there was a need for additional oversight and technical training to ensure uniformity among the various State programs. The Safety Board believes that the FTA should develop and implement an action plan, including provisions for technical and financial resources as necessary, to enhance the effectiveness of State safety oversight programs to identify safety deficiencies and to ensure that those deficiencies are corrected.

Train Evacuation

Instructions for emergencies are posted in each railcar. The instructions tell passengers to listen for instructions and wait on the train. Some passengers exited the train before they were given instructions to do so. Considering the arcing and smoke being generated at the end of the train, it is understandable that passengers in the rear of the train started exiting the train immediately.

According to the CTA's *Rail System Rule Book*, when a train goes into emergency the operator should notify the control center and attempt to find and correct the trouble. After CTA train number 220 went into emergency, the operator exited the control compartment and walked out onto the catwalk to determine what had happened. He saw thick smoke at the rear of the train and passengers on the catwalk. Using a portable two-way radio, he informed the rail controller of

---

[53] U.S. Government Accountability Office, *Rail Transit, Additional Federal Leadership Would Enhance FTA's State Safety Oversight Program,* Report to the Committee on Transportation and Infrastructure, House of Representative (Washington, DC: GAO, July 2006).

what was happening and went from car to car telling passengers to exit the train. He did not use the intercom to make a train-wide announcement because he had exited the train to assess the situation.

Once the operator had assessed the situation from the catwalk and decided to tell the passengers to exit the train, he could have reentered the control compartment and made an announcement via the intercom rather than running from car to car. Although more passengers would have heard such a train-wide announcement, the actions of the operator were not unreasonable considering how quickly events occurred immediately after the derailment. The operator was in regular contact with the control center using his portable radio, and he could be heard providing information to passengers about how to open the car doors and directing them toward the emergency exit. However, in response to postaccident questionnaires, some passengers stated that they did not hear the operator's instructions. Therefore, the Safety Board believes that the CTA should examine and improve, as necessary, its ability to communicate with passengers and perform emergency evacuations.

Tunnel Evacuation

During the early emergency response efforts, the personnel in the control center did not have specific information about the location of the accident train. The operator told the rail controller that his train had been headed northbound approaching Grand/Milwaukee. Based on this information, the power controller activated the emergency lights and announcements at the emergency exit immediately south of the Grand/Milwaukee station. Next, additional emergency exit lights and announcements were activated north of the Grand/Milwaukee station. The lights and announcements were not activated at the closest accessible emergency exit, 300 North Clinton Street, until 5:24 p.m.

Emergency call boxes are one way of determining a person's location, and subsequently a train's location, in a subway tunnel. The call boxes have unique identification numbers that can be used to locate the call box and its user. A passenger using a an emergency call box told the CTA power controller that he and other passengers were at box number 52379. The power controller should have been able to determine the location of that call box. Before the accident, however, the emergency call boxes were given new five-digit numbers. The subway maps in use at the time of the accident still had the old seven-digit box numbers. When the accident occurred, the subway maps were being revised. Since the accident, the CTA has revised and distributed its subway maps, and these maps now reflect the current location of all emergency call boxes and their identification numbers.

Initially, emergency responders did not have specific information about the location of the train. In the first call to 911, a passenger told a dispatcher that there was fire and smoke on the Blue Line, the train had derailed, and it was past Clark/

Lake. Based on this information, emergency responders were dispatched to the Clark/Lake station. As more information became available, emergency responders were told of different locations (for example, the Grand/Milwaukee station), and they began to respond to each location. The Safety Board concludes that because a train indication system had not been installed on the Dearborn Subway and the CTA's control center could not identify the location of an emergency call box used to report the accident, the specific location of train 220 could not be determined, which delayed the emergency response and the activation of emergency exit lights and announcements at the closest accessible emergency exit. The CTA has train indication systems on multiple lines that provide train locations to the control center. It reported that a signal replacement project that will provide train locations for the Dearborn Subway is on schedule for completion by 2009.

Tunnel Ventilation

The ability to fully and efficiently control all aspects of a ventilation system can play a pivotal role in removing smoke and aiding passenger evacuation during an emergency event. When fire, smoke, or fumes are present, CTA's standard practice is to confirm the location of an incident and the circumstances involved before activating ventilation. This helps ensure that the power controller knows which fans to turn on and in which direction the airflow will best assist with emergency response efforts.

CTA personnel in the northbound tunnel reported (by radio) that smoke was moving toward the Clark/Lake station. Upon receiving this information, the power controller initiated ventilation efforts to remove the smoke at 5:18 p.m., about 11 minutes after the accident. Initially, exhaust fan 133 was activated, then about 8 minutes later the Clark/Lake station under-platform fan, and all the Washington, Monroe, and Jackson continuous platform fans were operated in the exhaust mode. However, fan 133 was north of the accident site and the other fans were south of the accident site. As a result, the Safety Board concludes that the initial efforts to remove smoke were inefficient because the fans were pulling against each other from opposite sides of the smoke source.

CTA personnel later reported heavy smoke from the vent shaft for fan 108 just south of the accident site, and directed the power controller to put the under-platform fan at the Clark/Lake station and the under-platform fans at the Washington, Monroe, and Jackson stations' continuous platform into the supply mode. Once this was done, the smoke flowed northward through exhaust fan 133, and conditions inside the tunnel and stations improved greatly. However, because fan 133 was not reversible, the smoke had to be exhausted through it and northward in the same direction that people were moving to exit. The Safety Board concludes that had fan 133 been capable of dual direction (reversible), the smoke could have been removed in a direction opposite that of the path of evacuation. Exhaust fan 108, which had been removed in 2001, was located just to the south of the accident site. The Safety Board concludes that if fan 108 had been reinstalled and operational, the smoke could have been eliminated faster and in a direction opposite that of the path of evacuation.

During the accident response, the CTA found that fan 157 would not start. However, once the under-platform fans at the Clark/Lake station and the fans in the continuous platform at the Washington, Monroe, and Jackson stations were put into supply mode, fan 133 efficiently removed the smoke from the tunnel. Therefore, in this case, it does not appear that fan 157 would have appreciably improved the smoke removal process even if it had been operational.

Because of the problems encountered with ventilation of the smoke generated during the accident, the Safety Board believes that the CTA should perform a comprehensive computational study of the existing ventilation system using various fire and smoke scenarios to identify potential deficiencies, and make improvements to the ventilation system and smoke removal procedures based on the findings of the study. These actions should address reinstalling fan 108 and replacing unidirectional fans (including fan 133) with dual direction fans as needed. The Safety Board also believes that the FTA should inform all rail transit agencies about the circumstances of the July 11, 2006, CTA subway accident and urge them to examine and improve, as necessary, their ability to communicate with passengers and perform emergency evacuations from their tunnel systems, including the ability to (1) identify the exact location of a train, (2) locate a specific call box, and (3) remove smoke from their tunnel systems.

Conclusions

Findings

1. The following were not factors in the accident: the operator's qualifications, his operation of the train, or drug or alcohol use.

2. There was no preaccident mechanical or component failure on any of the train's cars.

3. The tie plates and fastener system failed to maintain the track gage because of the effects of corrosion and/or wear on the rails and rail fastener system, and degraded half-ties.

4. The dark area on the inner rail of the curve, the abrasion on the tie plates and ties, the broken lag screws, the tie plates' elongated fastener holes, and poor drainage in the area of the derailment were all readily observable and should have been documented during walking inspections.

5. Track inspectors in the Dearborn Subway did not have sufficient time allotted for inspecting all of their assigned territory twice a week as prescribed.

6. The Chicago Transit Authority track inspection training program did not adequately prepare inspectors to perform their required duties and it did not address the unique demands of inspecting and maintaining elevated track structures or track structures located inside tunnels.

7. The use of a track geometry strength and condition test vehicle would have simulated train loads and better identified areas of poor track gage and the need for corrective action.

8. Because the Chicago Transit Authority failed to establish an effective track inspection and maintenance program, unsafe track conditions and deficiencies were not corrected.

9. Because the Regional Transportation Authority failed to follow up with the Chicago Transit Authority and prompt action to correct safety deficiencies identified in the triennial report, unsafe track conditions continued to exist that should have been corrected.

10. The Federal Transit Administration's oversight of the Regional Transportation Authority's Rail Safety Oversight Program was inadequate and failed to

prompt actions needed to correct track safety deficiencies on the Chicago Transit Authority's rail transit system.

11. Because a train indication system had not been installed on the Dearborn Subway and the Chicago Transit Authority's control center could not identify the location of an emergency call box used to report the accident, the specific location of train 220 could not be determined, which delayed the emergency response and the activation of emergency exit lights and announcements at the closest accessible emergency exit.

12. The initial efforts to remove smoke were inefficient because the fans were pulling against each other from opposite sides of the smoke source.

13. Had fan 133 been capable of dual direction (reversible), the smoke could have been removed in a direction opposite that of the path of evacuation.

14. If fan 108 had been reinstalled and operational, the smoke could have been eliminated faster and in a direction opposite that of the path of evacuation.

Probable Cause

The National Transportation Safety Board determines that the probable cause of the July 11, 2006, derailment of Chicago Transit Authority train number 220 in the subway in Chicago, Illinois, was the Chicago Transit Authority's ineffective management and oversight of its track inspection and maintenance program and its system safety program, which resulted in unsafe track conditions. Contributing to the accident were the Regional Transportation Authority's failure to require that action be taken by the Chicago Transit Authority to correct unsafe track conditions and the Federal Transit Administration's ineffective oversight of the Regional Transportation Authority. Contributing to the seriousness of the accident was smoke in the tunnel and the delay in removing that smoke.

RECOMMENDATIONS

As a result of its investigation of the July 11, 2006, derailment of Chicago Transit Authority train number 220 in Chicago, Illinois, the National Transportation Safety Board makes the following safety recommendations:

To the Federal Transit Administration:

Modify your program to ensure that State safety oversight agencies take action to prompt rail transit agencies to correct all safety deficiencies that are identified as a result of oversight inspections and safety reviews, regardless of whether those deficiencies are labeled as "findings," "observations," or some other term. (R-07-9)

Develop and implement an action plan, including provisions for technical and financial resources as necessary, to enhance the effectiveness of State safety oversight programs to identify safety deficiencies and to ensure that those deficiencies are corrected. (R-07-10)

Schedule the Chicago Transit Authority as a priority for receiving the maintenance oversight workshop and the training course to be developed for track inspectors and supervisors that will address the unique demands of track inspection in the rail transit environment. (R-07-11)

Inform all rail transit agencies about the circumstances of the July 11, 2006, Chicago Transit Authority subway accident and urge them to examine and improve, as necessary, their ability to communicate with passengers and perform emergency evacuations from their tunnel systems, including the ability to (1) identify the exact location of a train, (2) locate a specific call box, and (3) remove smoke from their tunnel systems. (R-07-12)

To the State of Illinois:

Evaluate the Regional Transportation Authority's effectiveness, procedures, and authority, and take action to ensure that all safety deficiencies identified during rail transit safety inspections and reviews of the Chicago Transit Authority are corrected, regardless of whether those deficiencies are labeled as "findings," "observations," or some other term. (R-07-13)

To the Regional Transportation Authority:

Determine if track safety deficiencies on the Chicago Transit Authority's Dearborn Subway in the area of the derailment have been adequately repaired. (R-07-14)

Strengthen your followup action on Chicago Transit Authority system safety reviews to ensure that the Chicago Transit Authority corrects all identified safety deficiencies, regardless of whether those deficiencies are labeled as "findings," "observations," or some other term. (R-07-15)

To the Chicago Transit Board:

Direct the Chicago Transit Authority to correct all safety deficiencies identified by the Regional Transportation Authority in its most recent and future safety inspections and reviews, regardless of whether those deficiencies are labeled as "findings," "observations," or some other term. (R-07-16)

To the Chicago Transit Authority:

Correct all safety deficiencies identified by the Regional Transportation Authority in its most recent and future safety inspections and reviews, regardless of whether those deficiencies are labeled as "findings," "observations," or some other term. (R-07-17)

Examine all of the elements in the American Public Transportation Association's "Standard for Rail Transit Track Inspection and Maintenance" and incorporate all appropriate elements of this standard in your system safety program. Specifically, include the regular use of track geometry vehicle inspections and the inspection of rail for internal defects in your system safety program. (R-07-18)

Evaluate all territories to determine the number of inspectors and the amount of time needed to ensure that adequate track inspections are conducted, and implement appropriate changes. (R-07-19)

Schedule as a priority the maintenance oversight workshop and the training course that the Federal Transit Administration plans to develop for track inspectors and supervisors that will address the unique demands of track inspection in the rail transit environment. (R-07-20)

Perform a comprehensive computational study of the existing ventilation system using various fire and smoke scenarios to identify potential deficiencies, and make improvements to the ventilation system and smoke removal procedures based on the findings of the study. These actions should address reinstalling fan 108 and replacing unidirectional fans (including fan 133) with dual direction fans as needed. (R-07-21)

Examine and improve, as necessary, your ability to communicate with passengers and perform emergency evacuations. (R-07-22)

BY THE NATIONAL TRANSPORTATION SAFETY BOARD

Mark V. Rosenker
Chairman

Robert L. Sumwalt
Vice Chairman

Deborah A. P. Hersman
Member

Kathryn O'Leary Higgins
Member

Steven R. Chealander
Member

Adopted: September 11, 2007

Robert L. Sumwalt, Vice Chairman, filed the following concurring statement on September 13, 2007.

I applaud the staff's work on this accident and I fully support the report, findings, probable cause and recommendations that the Board unanimously adopted.

The report states that this was an "organizational accident." In the Board meeting to deliberate this accident, Gerald Weeks, Ph.D., chief of the human performance and survival factors division of NTSB's Office of Rail, Pipeline and Hazardous Materials, characterized this accident as a "case study in organizational accidents." This concurring statement is to provide additional information to support that notion.

I have long advocated a systems approach to accident investigation. Identifying this as an organizational accident is fully in line with that belief. A systems approach acknowledges that all components of the system must be examined to determine their potential role in the accident causation.

Active Failures and Latent Conditions

The report states, "The investigation found a series of latent conditions and active failures at many levels throughout the Chicago Transit Authority (CTA) corporate structure, which is characteristic of an organizational accident." The report quotes Dr. James Reason, saying, "organizational accidents have multiple causes involving many people operating at different levels of their respective companies."[1]

Dr. Reason believes that incidents and accidents in high-technology industries are rarely caused exclusively by mistakes or failures on the part of "front line operators."[2] Instead, Reason feels that the accidents often result from the interaction of active failures[3] (committed by front line operators) and a series of latent conditions that are embedded in the system.

Reason discusses the effects of latent conditions by stating, "Like pathogens, latent conditions – such as poor design, gaps in supervision, undetected manufacturing defects or maintenance failures, unworkable procedures, clumsy automation, shortfalls in training, less than adequate tools and equipment – may be present for many years before they combine with local circumstances and active failures to penetrate the system's many layers of defences. They arise from strategic and other top-level decisions made by governments, regulators, manufacturers, designers and organizational managers. The impact of these decisions spreads throughout the organization, shaping a distinctive corporate culture and creating error-producing factors within the individual workplaces."

Maurino, Reason, *et al*[4] say that latent organizational failures are "invariably the true root causes of accidents within high-technology industries," and they cite the following as examples of such:

- A lack of top-level management safety commitment or focus.

- The creation of conflicts between production and safety goals.

- Poor planning, communications, monitoring, control or supervision.

- Organizational deficiencies leading to blurred safety and administrative responsibilities.

---

[1] Reason. James. *Managing the Risks of Organizational Accidents.* (Burlington: Ashgate Publishing Company, 1997).

[2] Front line operators are those people who are performing the actual hands-on tasks, as opposed to managers who are further removed from the front line. Examples of front line operators include track inspectors, mechanics and train crew personnel. Examples of front line operators in other modes of transportation include pilots, air traffic controllers, harbor pilots and pipeline controllers.

[3] An active failure is an error or unsafe act that is introduced by front line operators.

[4] Maurino, D., Reason, J., Johnston, N., Lee, R., *Beyond Aviation Human Factors.* (Ashgate Publishing Company, 1995).

–   Deficiencies in training.

–   Poor maintenance management or control.

–   Monitoring failures by regulatory or safety agencies.

As shown below, each of these factors was present in this accident:

–   Inadequate inspection equipment

   o   At the time of the accident, CTA did not utilize a track geometry vehicle or internal rail defect detection equipment, although such equipment was in use with virtually all other rail transit agencies in this country.
   o   Inadequate lighting to illuminate the track structure to facilitate inspections.

–   Conflicting demands on track inspectors

   o   In addition to performing track inspections, the inspectors were required to perform rail repairs on areas that they identified as needing repair. This created the conflict between detecting problems that they would later be required to repair.

   o   Combining maintenance and inspection functions has the potential to compromise Quality Assurance. Many organizations ensure Quality Assurance by requiring maintenance and inspection to be separate functions.

–   Improper prioritization of track inspections

   o   If an important maintenance situation occurred, the section roadmaster would halt the inspections and utilize inspectors to make the necessary repairs.

–   Budget pressures

   o   Fewer maintenance personnel were employed due to budget constraints, which, in some cases, caused track inspectors to be used to perform maintenance instead of inspecting track.

–   Inadequate staffing

   o   The section roadmaster said that he, the track engineer IV maintenance (his immediate supervisor), and the manager of track had inspected the tunnel area where the derailment occurred and they all agreed that the "area was bad," but staff was not available to make permanent repairs.

- o If an inspector was absent from work, required inspection would not occur.

– Improper repairs

- o Track spikes were used instead of lag screws, which compromised the electrical insulation of the rail and accelerated the corrosive process.

– Inadequate time to perform required track inspections

- o Inspectors did not have sufficient time allotted for inspecting all of their assigned territory twice a week as prescribed.

– Falsification of inspections records

- o Inspection reports showed that entire track territory was inspected, even though it was not inspected.

– Incomplete records

- o In the three months prior to the accident, more than 80 percent of the track inspection records for the Blue Line territory were missing.

- o Some track defects were noted but there were no parallel records to show the repairs were made.

- o Roadmasters were not reviewing records in accordance with CTA procedure.

– Required supervisory inspections not done

- o The section roadmaster conducted only one monthly inspection in the five months prior to the accident, although these inspections should have been conducted every month.

– Inadequate training

- o Inspector training and experience requirements were significantly lower than other rail transit agencies.

- o Inspector classroom training did not cover procedures for inspections conducted in tunnels or on elevated structures, although 50 percent of CTA's track structure was in tunnels or on elevated tracks.

- Inadequate internal evaluation program

  o System Safety personnel were responsible for reviewing the track inspection and maintenance program, but they did not perform this role, nor did they have the technical track expertise to perform those functions.

- Inadequate regulatory oversight

  o The Regional Transit Authority (RTA) did not follow-up with CTA and prompt action to correct identified track deficiencies.

  o The Federal Transit Administration (FTA) did not provide adequate oversight of RTA's Rail Safety Oversight Program which led to uncorrected track deficiencies.

When combined, these latent organizational factors are highly indicative of a system that placed insufficient priority on and attention to track inspection and maintenance.

Reason's "Swiss Cheese" Model

A robust system has multiple layers of defense to guard against undesired outcomes. James Reason says that latent conditions place holes in these layers of defense, which allows the layers of defense to look like Swiss cheese.

There were several layers of defense to guard against accidents such as the July 11, 2006 CTA accident. Such layers of defense included front line track inspectors properly performing their jobs; supervisors adequately overseeing the work of the inspectors; management establishing and maintaining a safety culture where track inspection and maintenance receive proper attention through dedication of resources; and regulatory agency oversight.

Unfortunately, each of these layers of defense (barriers) had holes that were created by active failures and latent conditions. The visual picture portrayed here is that each of the layers of Swiss cheese had holes; when the holes aligned, an accident trajectory was allowed to penetrate each barrier through the holes, thus enabling the accident.

For any given accident there are typically more latent conditions than active failures. In this accident, the active failure was the track inspectors not properly inspecting track. However, only addressing active failures leaves latent conditions embedded in the system waiting to ensnare another unsuspecting front line operator.

Addressing latent conditions offers the greatest potential for safety improvements. Unfortunately, latent conditions are often more difficult to identify and therefore, are often not found and corrected.

Organizational expert Dan Maurino said, "Error should be considered like fever: an indication of illness rather than its cause." I am quite pleased that the Safety Board's investigation of this CTA accident did not stop with identifying the fever — the active failure of the track inspectors properly performing their jobs. Doing so would have accomplished nothing to actually improve safety, as the numerous other deficiencies or latent conditions would have remained undetected and uncorrected in the system.

I found this accident report to be thorough, coherent and well written. I hope to see continued emphasis on taking a systems approach to identifying both active failures and latent conditions in future accident investigations.

Chairman Rosenker and Member Chealander joined Vice Chairman Sumwalt in this statement.

Kathryn O'Leary Higgins, Member, filed the following concurring statement on September 18, 2007.

I concur with this important report. I believe the staff's hard work and this concise report of their comprehensive investigation should serve as a wake-up call not only to the second largest transit system in the country, but to all transit agencies who transport millions of passengers every year with equipment and infrastructure that ages with each passing day. This accident is a clear demonstration of the need to understand an aging system and to invest in maintaining the safety of that system.

For me, as the Board Member on scene for this accident, one of the most compelling issues was the CTA operator's inability to communicate effectively with the passengers on train 220 during the evening rush hour emergency. As outlined in CTA publication number 7039 (04-30-00), it is the train operator's duty to:

1. Call the controller and request assistance. Advise that an evacuation appears to be necessary and if power will have to be removed.

2. Communicate to the controller all pertinent information relative to the evacuation: location, closest exit, etc).

3. Communicate to the passengers what is happening and why before leaving the motorcab, using both interior and exterior speakers.

4. Request that passengers familiarize themselves with the emergency evacuation procedures posted in each car.

5. Make certain that the announcements are communicated to all passengers by walking through the entire train repeating the announcements.

There are additional procedures the operator is to follow in communicating with and evacuating passengers under a variety of circumstances. The operator of the accident train could only complete the first step in this list because he exited the train to try to determine what caused the train to stop. His ability to identify the precise location of the train and the nearest exit was hampered by the lack of clear markers in the tunnel. When he left the train, he lost his ability to communicate over the speakers with his passengers and inform them of the actions they should take.

As the press accounts at the time of the accident made clear, this lack of information was very upsetting to many of the passengers. According to the account of one passenger, she "waited for some kind of direction, perhaps a voice over a public address system, anything. The smoke was bad, and within minutes she and her fellow passengers decided to get out and start walking. Some weren't sure that was the best thing to do, but eventually everyone agreed.... Some people were getting panicky. They pried the door open and began stepping onto a narrow ledge...."

The signs posted on the doors of the train cars instruct passengers not to open the doors. Fortunately everyone made it to the emergency exit. The operator did the best he could to point everyone in the right direction. While there were injuries, we can be thankful that they were not more serious and that there were no fatalities. A more serious accident could have had a very different outcome.

Once the operator left the cab he could communicate with the controller over his hand-held radio but he could no longer communicate over the intercom with the passengers to provide directions and assistance. I believe the operator should not have to choose between communicating with the command center and communicating with passengers who need his immediate attention. The instructions for the operator in CTA's Rail System Rule Book are contradictory and in this accident the operator could not comply with all of them. The operator is to be commended for doing his best under very difficult circumstances. He stayed in the tunnel until the last passenger was evacuated.

CTA has an obligation to its operators and its passenger to make sure that in the event of an accident, emergency evacuation safety instructions can be given and followed. That requires a communications system that allows the operator to inform both the passengers and the command center about the event and to instruct passengers on the fastest and safest way to exit the train and reach the emergency exit.

This accident offers many lessons to both CTA and to rail transit systems around the country and we have made a number of recommendations to address those issues. In particular, we have asked the Federal Transit Administration to inform all rail transit agencies of the circumstances of this accident so that they can improve their emergency evacuation procedures, including communication with passengers. We have asked CTA to do the same. I hope both CTA and FTA will take these recommendations to heart and move expeditiously to implement them.

Chairman Rosenker, Vice Chairman Sumwalt, and Member Chealander joined Member Higgins in this statement.

APPENDIX A

Investigation

The National Response Center notified the National Transportation Safety Board of the Chicago Transit Authority accident about 7:30 p.m., eastern daylight time, on July 11, 2006. The investigator-in-charge and other members of the Safety Board investigative team were launched from the Washington, D.C., headquarters office and from the Chicago, Illinois, and Gardena, California, field offices. Investigative groups were established to study operations, track and signals, mechanical, survival factors, human performance, government oversight, fire, and metallurgy issues. Member Kathryn O'Leary Higgins was the Board Member on scene.

Parties to the investigation included the Chicago Transit Authority, the Regional Transportation Authority, the city of Chicago, and the Amalgamated Transit Union.

APPENDIX B

**Federal Transit Administration May 8, 2007, Letter Addressing
Track Worker Protection and Maintenance Oversight Issues**

U.S. Department
of Transportation

**Federal Transit
Administration**

Administrator

400 Seventh St., S.W.
Washington, D.C. 20590

MAY 8 2007

Subject: Track Worker Protection and Maintenance Oversight

Dear Colleague:

Over the last 18 months, 11 track workers have lost their lives in accidents that occurred on the nation's heavy rail and commuter rail systems. More than a dozen track workers have been seriously injured. While rail transit remains among the safest modes of transportation, I am concerned by the escalating number of incidents involving our transit employees nationwide.

Between October 2005 and April 2007, the Federal Transit Administration (FTA) and the Federal Railroad Administration (FRA) data show a three-fold increase in the number of rail transit worker fatalities and a significant increase in injuries. While the most serious accidents have occurred at a handful of agencies, we are all vulnerable when our industry's employees are placed at risk.

As a show of solidarity with the agencies that have experienced these accidents, I urge the Executive Directors and General Managers at each of our heavy rail and commuter rail agencies to immediately request a briefing regarding what their agencies are doing to protect workers. Critical issues involved in recent accidents include failure to notify dispatchers and operators of the location of work crews, failure to establish adequate work site clearance plans, failure to conduct adequate on-site track safety job briefings, failure of operators to follow speed restrictions, and failure of work crew leaders to remain at the site.

I also urge our State Safety Oversight Program Managers to contact the rail transit agencies in their jurisdictions to review current track worker protection programs. Only through strong management commitment and vigilant oversight can we ensure the protection of our employees, who put their lives on the line to keep our systems safe and secure.

FTA Initiatives

In the coming months, FTA will be implementing new initiatives to address track worker protection and maintenance oversight issues. These initiatives focus on three areas:

- Technical Assistance
- Training & Outreach
- Research

Technical Assistance

In late 2006, FTA identified its "Top 10 Safety Action Priorities" as part of its *Rail Transit Safety Action Plan*. FTA also conducted a joint study with FRA on commuter rail safety issues. Both of these documents are available on FTA's website at: http://transit-safety.volpe.dot.gov/Publications/order/default.asp#Safety). Two of FTA's Top 10 Safety Action Priorities directly relate to track worker protection and the enhanced oversight of maintenance activities. FTA will soon be updating its safety and security website to provide information, guidance, standards, templates, and recommended practices for addressing each of these Top 10 Priorities.

In the interim, specifically for track inspection and track worker protection issues, FTA urges interested parties to review the following:

American Public Transportation Association (APTA)
http://www.aptastandards.com/PublishedStandards/Rail/tabid/84/Default.aspx

- APTA Rail Transit Standard for Work Zone Safety, RT-S-OP- 004-03
- APTA Rail Transit Standard for Transit Track Inspection and Maintenance, RTS-FS-002-02
- APTA Recommended Practice Recommended Practice for Wayside AC Signal Power System Inspection and Testing, APTA-RT-RP-SC-001-02
- APTA Recommended Practice for Wayside DC Signal Power System Inspection and Testing, APTA-RT-RP-SC-002-02

American Railway Engineering and Maintenance of Way Association (AREMA)
http://www.arema.org/eseries/scriptcontent/index.cfm

- Manual for Railway Engineering, including Volume 1 Track, Chapter 5 and Volume 3, Infrastructure and Passenger, Chapter 12, Rail Transit.

Federal Railroad Administration (FRA)
http://www.access.gpo.gov/nara/cfr/waisidx_03/49cfr213_03.html

- 49 CFR 213, Track Safety Standards

http://www.fra.dot.gov/downloads/Safety/life_tips.pdf

- Roadway Worker Protection Life Tips

Training & Outreach

To support the needs of industry, FTA will be conducting workshops and training specifically aimed at identifying and resolving the underlying causes that contribute to these accidents.

- Maintenance Oversight Workshops: Many of our heavy rail transit agencies are struggling with looming budget deficits, increasing demands for revenue service, and extensive capital investment programs to upgrade aging infrastructure. In managing these challenging issues, there are a number of inter-related and complex factors that limit:

  o The resources available to perform maintenance,
  o The training available for maintenance and operations personnel,
  o The access of maintenance personnel to track under non-revenue service conditions, and
  o The integration of technology into track inspection and maintenance practices.

  Over the next 18 months, at each of the nation's 13 heavy rail transit agencies, FTA plans to conduct a 2-day workshop with maintenance, operations and safety personnel and with executive leadership to explore these challenges and to attempt to identify possible options for improvement. FTA plans to use these workshops to galvanize the attention of industry on maintenance issues. These workshops will also support the development of guidelines on improved maintenance practices in the heavy rail environment.

- Track Inspection Training: Over the next year, FTA plans to develop a training course specifically for track inspectors and supervisors, to address the unique demands of track inspection in the rail transit environment. This course will incorporate elements of FRA's 49 CFR Part 213, as well as APTA's rail transit standards and the AREMA guidance. This course will initially be offered at the nation's 13 heavy rail transit agencies. Over time, FTA will expand this course to commuter rail agencies and light rail agencies.

- Safety and Security Roundtables: Beginning with the next Safety and Security Roundtable in July in Chicago, FTA will actively engage participants in discussions and presentations related to track worker protection and maintenance oversight issues. FTA urges safety representatives to attend this July workshop and to bring with them their ideas, concerns, and challenges.

- TransitWatch: FTA is working to update the TransitWatch program to include safety issues for employees and passengers. Through this new initiative, transit agencies will have templates, brochures, posters and other materials available to support adherence to safety rules and to prevent at-risk behavior.

- Outreach with Executive Leadership: In partnership with the National Transportation Safety Board (NTSB) and APTA, FTA will be conducting outreach with Executive Directors and General Managers regarding track worker protection and maintenance oversight issues during upcoming APTA conferences.

Research

FTA will continue its partnership with APTA in the Rail Transit Standards Program to identify and address issues raised as a result of the Maintenance Oversight Workshops and the Track Inspection Training. Wherever possible, FTA looks to partner with APTA in developing consensus-based standards as the best form of technical assistance to industry.

FTA will also continue to sponsor research through the Transportation Research Board, Transit Cooperative Research Program and the University Transportation Centers. There are opportunities to use available technology to enhance the safety of track workers, to improve the identification, tracking and prioritization of maintenance issues, and to integrate materials testing and quality assurance/quality control practices more effectively into transit maintenance programs.

Conclusion

As an industry, we are confronting a serious set of issues that challenge our abilities to protect employees and ensure the safety and reliability of our infrastructure. I thank you for your on-going efforts to partner with FTA in meeting these challenges.

Sincerely,

James S. Simpson